ONE MORE RESCUE

One More Rescue
From a Devastating Accident to Freeing Children from Human Trafficking

This book is set in the typeface *Athelas* designed by Veronika Burian and Jose Scaglione.

Paperback ISBN: 979-8-3209-3477-8

A Publication of *Tall Pine Books*
119 E Center Street, Suite B4A | Warsaw, Indiana 46580
www.tallpinebooks.com

| 1 24 24 20 16 02 |

Published in the United States of America

NICOLE MASON FITZPATRICK
with Shelley Chapman

ONE

MORE

RESCUE

FROM A DEVASTATING ACCIDENT
TO FREEING CHILDREN FROM
HUMAN TRAFFICKING

"Such an incredible, beautiful, and inspiring story of a real-life superhero. Nicole is a light shining in the darkness. God uses her to save the lives of the most innocent. Everyone needs to read this!"

—Dr. Angela Ruark
Educator, Writer and Editor

"In the world of NGOs and individuals striving to aid children, few match the remarkable impact of Nicole and her husband. They epitomize the gold standard for reaching children, not only achieving significant impact but also fostering incredible outcomes that glorify God. May God bless them abundantly for their dedication and the positive results of their work. I urge you to read this book and glean crucial insights from their journey. It offers a profound understanding of both the challenges and victories inherent in such endeavors driven by genuine compassion. I am immensely grateful to God for Nicole, her husband, and the invaluable lessons this book imparts."

—Victor Marx
Founder of *All Things Possible Ministries*,
Humanitarian and Filmmaker

Dedicated to my constant source of unconditional love and support, my husband Jason.

And to our two beautiful, strong and always caring children, Sed and Jasmine.

Together, with God, we built it all.

ACKNOWLEDGEMENTS

This endeavor would not have been possible without the encouragement of so many people.

I would like to give my warmest thanks to every person who motivated me to write a book, both after the tragic accident and amnesia, then once I began rescuing innocent lives from the atrocities of human trafficking. My most sincere thanks to my family, friends and donors for their faithful support in prayer and finances. I'd like to give a special thanks to Bruce and Cathy Wagner for their long term support that has helped us build so many churches, Homes and rehabs.

I want to acknowledge and give my warmest thanks to all of my wonderful family: especially my mom, dad, stepdad, my two sisters and my bonus sister, my two brothers and three bonus brothers. I thank my husband's family, all my friends, my sweet forever friend from childhood who has walked me through all of this, Jena Lindsey; and my co-workers and supporters, for their guidance, patience, advice and prayers as I pursued this journey.

I also wish to acknowledge Beatrice Bruno; thank you for helping me begin this journey of telling my story, for listening to me and researching details.

I would like to give a very special thanks to Britt and Audrey Hancock, for persistently encouraging me to write, and then helping edit the final piece.

Words cannot express my gratitude to Maighel Grisolle, who also encouraged me and introduced me to Shelley Chapman. Without these encounters, this book probably would never have happened. My deepest and most profound gratitude to you, Shelley, for knitting together so well my 334-page first draft, plus all my other thoughts and stories, into these pages. I am eternally grateful to you.

Finally, I would like to thank my King Jesus, for being with me every step of the way, as He promised me, through all the difficulties, betrayals, threats, risks, and hardships. I have experienced His guidance day by day, and for that, I can never thank Him enough.

NICOLE MASON FITZPATRICK

CONTENTS

FOREWORD

I WALKED INTO the hospital room and looked at Nicole. A metal "halo" was screwed into her skull to keep her head still. Her brown hair was beautiful and she gave a sweet sleepy smile. I smiled back and laid my hand on her arm. My eyes filled with tears. It was a miracle she was alive after the accident and it would be an ongoing miracle for her to recover.

In February 1987, my husband, Britt, met Nicole's family when she was 13 years old; I met them two years later. We had prayed for them for six years, but now the prayers were of a different fervency. This was a matter of life and death. Miraculously, Nicole lived!

And, oh what a life Nicole Fitzpatrick has lived!! Not an ordinary life — an extraordinary one! Extraordinary, yet not easy.

She and her husband, Jason, have taken the Gospel to villages in 10 states and gone head-to-head with witchdoctors, cartels and sex trafficking lords. She has rescued, raised, and restored over 2000 children from abject poverty, abandonment, abuse and sex trafficking. Their horrific stories rob my sleep. Their victories make me happy cry.

Nicole and I have many shared memories since 1990. We have laughed together, cried together, been frustrated and irritated and excited and exhausted. Real. Our families have worked side by side as pioneer missionaries in hard to reach places in the mountains and valleys of Mexico. I was in the delivery room when her daughter was born. Our children played together. We sat next to each other on small benches in tiny houses made of bamboo, and we have danced and worshiped side by side with sweat running down our backs and a smile on our faces.

In 2019, Nicole and Jason asked if they could become a part of Mountain Gateway, the ministry Britt and I founded. We are so very grateful that they became an affiliate ministry under us and that we are still a part of their story after so many years of friendship. It is an honor to walk beside them on this journey.

I invite you into Nicole's story. Hers is a story of determination, fortitude, and victory. She fought to regain what was lost in the accident and has gained even more. She's shown what true courage is - not an absence of fear - but right action in the face of the fear that she's had.

As you read *this book* you will be challenged to believe. Believe in the power of love. Believe in the power of obedience. Believe in God. You will see what God can do with someone who is willing, someone who said YES.

Shining His Light,

AUDREY HANCOCK
Co-founder of *Mountain Gateway*
www.MountainGateway.org

PREFACE

AS I SIT here at my office desk, listening to the soft rain coming gently down as it does almost daily in the deep Puebla mountains, and I look at all these pages before me, I am humbled and blessed, beyond what I have ever dreamed. This book has been so many years in the making; there have been many ideas about how to undertake it, many unfinished attempts.

At first, it was my closest friends and family who motivated me, during and after the wreck and my amnesia, and as I began to put my life back together. They saw me in my deepest struggles - tied to a bed, struggling with depression. They helped me to learn how to live again. My husband patiently waited for me when I felt I'd never met him before ... each and every day. I had no idea where I was, nor who I was. Had you told me back then that I would ever write a book, I do not think I would ever have believed you.

But now, decades later, it's a lot more than that.

It was about 20 years ago when I started my first rescues, and soon after my husband and I began the Village Children's Home. Over the years people from many nations have come to visit and stay a few days or weeks. They would constantly tell me, "You should write a book! People need to hear the story of your life and what you're doing!" Others would tell me to send some of the cases to *Law and Order*.

It was this encouragement that got me thinking that perhaps I really should write a book. And I am grateful that, after so long, it has finally become a reality.

The final product which you hold in your hands is a true labor of love. It is my hope that it will do a lot more than just entertain - that it will open your eyes to the world around you and show you God's heart for the weak and vulnerable; and that it will inspire you to obey Jesus, in whatever it is He wants you to do.

INTRODUCTION

"One can give without loving, but one cannot love without giving." - *Amy Carmichael*

IN READING A book that deals with the subject of child trafficking, you might be concerned, understandably, that this book will contain grisly details you'd prefer not to read or recommend to others. My hope is that, while tackling such a difficult subject head-on, I have been able to do so without revealing morbid details that may cause undue anguish.

This book will take you briefly through my childhood in the deep south of Louisiana and my early days with my husband; then through the tragic wreck and all that this involved. It will take you through just a few of the physical, mental, spiritual, and emotional struggles that I suffered in those early years.

But don't be afraid - it mainly concentrates on the positive, the many miracles that I can't deny God did for me. The many times I had to say "yes", over and over, to the unknown. And the hundreds of times that God kept His word and stayed by my side every step of the way.

It will take you through how I could only survive one day at a time in the hospital in Corpus Christi, Texas, to the beginnings of rescuing one child at a time in Tenango de las Flores,

Mexico. One more day ... one more child. You will see the circumstances that brought me to where I am now, having rescued and cared for over 2,000 children to date.

You will read stories of some of the children God allowed my team and I to rescue, from the atrocities of child porn, child sex trafficking, orphanhood, abandonment, and abuse at its worst. One of the big questions over the years has been "Which of all the crazy, unbelievable stories should I include?" I have indeed included a number of them. They might seem crazy and unbelievable, but they are all true. And strangely enough, there always seems to be something even crazier just around the corner.

Yes, I have seen the worst of humanity - but I have also seen the very best of humanity as we've joined hands to rescue these children. I have experienced firsthand the unconditional love of our Father - but also His just right hand with perpetrators and pedophiles.

My hope and prayer is that my story will inspire you to believe in our Savior for eternal life, and that in, for and through Him, you can and will do great things! I want to suggest to you that, after reading each chapter, you take time to reflect on what you have read. Was there something that impacted or challenged you? Is there something God is speaking to you to do or change? Make notes of your thoughts, and turn them into prayers - and action.

May you be blessed as you read my story. May God reveal Himself to you as the One who loves to rescue ... one more.

Amnesia

My soul, wait in silence for God alone, For my hope is from Him. - Psalm 62:5 (NASB)

Hardships often prepare ordinary people for an extraordinary destiny. - C.S. Lewis

" ...CONFIDENT OF THIS very thing, that He who began a good work among you will complete it by the day of Christ Jesus..."[1]

The words faded into my head as I gained consciousness. I didn't know who was speaking. I felt giddy, almost seasick, and my head throbbed. Where was I? I opened my eyes for a brief moment and saw a white ceiling. I sensed I was lying down and couldn't move. There were a number of regular beeps, quiet electronic sounds.

The voice continued: "... since both in my imprisonment and in the defense and confirmation of the gospel, you all are

---

1. Philippians 1:6, NASB

partakers of grace with me ..."[2] It was the Bible; somehow I realized that. It was disconcerting to hear the calm, soothing male voice reading the Scriptures, and at the same time to feel motion sick and trapped, unable to get up or move.

Someone else entered the room and came close to me - an unknown woman dressed in a blue uniform. Feeling my restraint, I tried to cry out, "Don't hurt me! Go away!" but no noise came from my voice.

I realized with alarm I had a tube in my throat. The woman in blue observed me carefully, made some changes to some tubes attached to me, wrote some things down in a file, and walked away. My mattress moved gently to the right. I felt like I was tied to the bed. My head began to pound.

Where was I? What was going on? What were they doing to me?

And as I realized I could not answer any of these questions, I also became aware that neither could I answer an even greater one. *Who was I?*

I drifted in and out of sleep, sometimes opening my eyes, other times awake and listening but with my eyes closed. I heard people praying for me; people coming to talk about me; other times that male voice reading the Bible. Not knowing who he was but feeling comforted by his voice, I could hear him say to me, "Nod once for yes, two for no." But my head was restrained and I couldn't move. Instead, I'd squeeze his hand holding mine, then fall asleep again.

I opened my eyes again; out of the corner of my eye I saw a woman in a gray uniform! I was definitely being tortured! I must be in some sort of POW camp or medical army center! At this point I panicked, trying to move my body and yelling "Let me out of here! Klinger! Hawkeye! Help me!" - but I still couldn't move, and my yells came out a whisper. The woman bent close

---

2. Philippians 1:7, NASB

to my face to hear what I was saying, then turned to a handsome young man who'd entered the room holding a pizza box and said to him, "I think she's saying *Klinger* and *Hawkeye* ...?" The man looked blank, and I remembered nothing more.

The next time I woke, I could see another woman with wavy black hair sitting by my bed. As I stirred she smiled, tiny dimples forming in both cheeks, and touching my hand she said gently, "Hey honey, how're you doing today?" She seemed like a nice person; she had kind eyes. But I had no idea who she was.

"What's going on?" I rasped. "Where am I?" I could feel the tube in my throat which stopped me from speaking normally.

Her voice was calm. "Nicole, you were in a truck accident. You were hurt very badly. You're in the hospital now. We're going to try to get you better."

"Has the guard gone?" I whispered fearfully. The woman looked confused. "The prison guard. Hot Lips Houlihan," I breathed out softly, trying to clarify things, but not even understanding why I said that.

She frowned, considering the words slowly. Then she said, "Nicole, that was a TV show called *M*A*S*H*. That's not real. You're not there. You're in a hospital in Corpus Christi. They're not guards, they're nurses. They're here to take care of you."

I looked at her as my mattress moved slowly to the right. "Who am I?" I asked her, feeling sick.

She squeezed my hand. "You're Nicole," she replied with a smile. "I'm your Mama. You had an accident. Look, this is Jason." She looked up at the tall young man who'd just entered the room. His face lit up when he saw me awake.

I whispered, "Hello, Doctor Jason." Even in my restrained state I felt content in some small way to have such a nice-looking doctor to attend to me.

His face fell. Approaching my bed, he took my hand in his,

looked at me searchingly and replied, "I'm not a doctor, Nicole; I'm your husband, Jason. See, I've got your wedding ring."

This was too much for my mind to comprehend. I wasn't old enough to be married! I was just a kid - wasn't I? I couldn't remember anything about being married. I didn't know this man at all! I attempted to pull my hand from his. I saw the expression on Jason's face - disbelief, hurt and disappointment all rolled into one. I didn't mean to hurt him. I closed my wet eyes, and drifted back into the calm state of sedation.

Several weeks continued of this sleeping and waking. Each time I woke, I thought I was in a POW camp or an episode of *M*A*S*H*, not knowing who I was or how long I'd been in this state, not knowing why I had eight tubes attached to machines, why I felt so much excruciating pain in so many parts of my body, or why the bed would oscillate back and forth. I didn't recognize anyone who came into the room to visit or to check up on me.

I woke numerous times a day; each time my Mom, Dad, or Jason would introduce themselves again, tell me my name and try to explain to me what had happened. But it had been so traumatic, such a horrific accident, that my brain had simply shut down and removed all memory - not only of the accident, but also of my past - in order to work on recovering from the enormous impact. All it could hold onto in these early weeks was an old TV show I used to watch with my Daddy when I was 4 years old. Everything else was completely gone.

I woke up again. I could tell I was in a different room, but I still had many tubes attached to me. I hated those tubes - I wanted to pull them all out. My back and my abdomen throbbed and ached. I looked around; there was a younger boy, around 10 years old, sitting on the end of the other bed in the room, watching TV absently, with a sad look on his face.

I knew who he was - he was my younger brother Lucas. I

looked at his face and felt sad too. I said, "Lucas, Bubba, what happened? Why are you in the hospital?"

Lucas turned the TV down, and turned to look at me. He rolled his eyes as if to say, "Here we go again", took a deep breath, and said, "I'm not in the hospital, sis. *You* are. You got in a wreck and were thrown from the truck." He began to explain things about me I did not know.

As we began to talk, a young man and an older woman entered the room. They looked familiar, but I couldn't quite remember their names. The woman sat down near my bed; the man stood at the foot of my bed, watching me as Lucas and I talked. He said to the woman, "Something's changed ... I see it in her eyes. Mrs. Liz - she knows who Lucas is! I've gotta tell the nurse!" He spun around and left the room.

When he came back in, the man asked me, "Do you remember me, Nicole?"

I whispered in reply, "Yes. You're the nurse."

"No, I'm not. I'm your husband, Jason!" he replied. He sounded frustrated. He walked over to the woman and asked me, "Who is this?"

I looked at her - there was something comforting about her. I replied, "I know her."

"Yes, you do know her. Who is she?"

"She's my Mama."

Mama's eyes shone as she gave a small smile and said, "Thank you, Lord." She'd seen me in my most broken state, on the edge of death, in the Intensive Care Unit. She'd been told by doctors many times over the weeks that I would definitely not survive my massive injuries. Then she'd been told I would remain in a vegetative state, living on life support for the rest of my life.

She kept faithfully praying and trusting in the Lord, and, it turned out, hundreds more were also faithfully praying for me.

And so, after several weeks of being in ICU and having multiple surgeries, I began rehabilitation.

Like a young plant suddenly grabbed and ripped out of the ground, my life had been totally uprooted. And yet God saw fit to keep me alive and on the long road to recovery.

The nurses and doctors from ICU were astounded, and often said so.

"How is it even possible she survived?"

CHAPTER ONE

Firmly Grounded

Train up a child in the way he should go, even when he grows older he will not abandon it. - Proverbs 22:6 (NASB)

We only have two choices: do nothing, or do something. - Tony Kirwan

I STILL DON'T remember much from my past. I've pieced together memories and moments over the years from photos people showed me, stories told by family and friends, smells that triggered a memory, and even from dreams. Slowly my mind began to heal and recall.

What I remember is happiness and innocence. We were a very happy family. My Dad was of mainly Scottish-Irish descent, and my Mom is Cajun French. I was born in 1974, just one year after my sister Christina; then came my brothers Robert and Lucas a few years later.

I was born in Baton Rouge and raised in nearby towns in South Louisiana; a warm, humid, spacious region of the U.S. filled with lush grass and historical live oaks, with the beloved Mississippi River meandering through. It was the true South, where children were brought up to speak respectfully to adults, using *Ma'am* and *Sir*.

I was my Daddy's girl, watching war movies and shows like *M*A*S*H* and *The Six Million Dollar Man* with him. I was a tomboy; if I wasn't running, I was riding my bike or motorcycle or learning to drive a 4WD. I loved athletics, kickball, volleyball, and baseball. I can remember painting eggs with my grandparents for Easter, playing horseshoes with my godfather, and having beautiful Christmas parties as a family.

As a child, when I'd have nightmares and would wake up frightened and crying, my Mama would always come into my bedroom, rub my back calmly and sing "Amazing Grace", and I'd be comforted. Even though my Dad wasn't a believer at the time, we were at church every time the doors were open.

My Mom and Dad were foster parents. We often had older kids coming in and out of our home. It was not just our nuclear family; it was communal living. It wasn't always easy - there were lots of disruptive moments - but for me, it seemed like a totally natural, normal thing to have other kids around who weren't my siblings by blood, cared for by my parents.

There is one thing that everyone who's ever known me all agrees on: I have *always* loved children. From the time the adults let me (when I was about eight or nine years old), I volunteered to look after the babies in our church nursery. I thrived on babysitting and children's church.

I watched a program once on Compassion International - a Christian ministry that "release[s] children out of poverty in Jesus' name"[1] - and decided then and there that I wanted to help children across the world who couldn't help themselves. I wanted to be their voice, their hands, their feet. Even before I was ten years old, God gave me a calling to hold onto for my whole life: the roots of that purpose would not be seen for many years, as they were deep and strong.

When I was small, I gave my life to Jesus. Even though I was little, I took this decision very seriously. When I was nine years old, I got baptized in the massive swimming pool at the house of a brother from our church, to show the commitment I'd made to follow Jesus Christ.

At that same time, my Daddy gave his life to Jesus, and his life was transformed. He very quickly became a street evangelist, preaching downtown in Baton Rouge and on Bourbon Street in New Orleans. He was an amazing preacher! People would listen to him and give their hearts to Jesus. Up until that year, I'd suffered from asthma, then when my Daddy got saved, he asked God to heal me - and He did! It grounded my faith in God not only as a loving Father, but also as all-powerful.

A few years later, when I was almost 13, my parents met David and Debbie Hogan, the founders of Freedom Ministries. This organization went into unreached indigenous villages and regions, mainly in Mexico. They shared the gospel, trained local pastors and leaders, and prayed for salvation, healing and deliverance to establish the kingdom of God in remote regions.[2]

David was a tall man with a goatee that became quite famous in many circles. He had a serious expression and an impressive presence whenever he came into the room. Debbie, his devoted wife, was always kind and smiling, and had a servant heart. David and Debbie came to our house and spoke to my parents about the importance of missions and the opportunities to spread the gospel in Latin America.

Dad and Mom were inspired, and obeyed the call to go - and everything changed after that. They joined Freedom Ministries and we spent a year in Texas at a Spanish language school. Then we all moved to the mission field: almost two years in Guatemala, almost a year in Mexico, then finally further south to Peru, which was where my Dad had wanted to work from the start. In our first year in Peru, my parents adopted a newborn baby girl, whom we named Hannah Raquel - my beautiful younger sister.

There was nothing simple about moving from the USA to Latin American countries. Before we left, my sister and I were taken aside by well-meaning people from our church who warned us of the danger we would face as pretty white teenagers. My parents didn't know about this at the time, but I remember being frightened about going into a completely unknown culture as a white American family.

In one sense, it was true - life as we knew it completely changed. Taking four kids to the mission field to minister in a different language and in different cultures was pretty tough. While my peers in the USA were doing normal Christian stuff like going to school, hanging out with friends, and going to youth group, I was walking through the jungles of Guatemala and waking up early to pray.

The example of obedience that my parents set for us kids gave me another root that grounded my impressionable teenage life - the understanding that being a Christian meant serving as Jesus served on this earth, not living for myself. I am so thankful to the Lord for this opportunity to go as a missionary family, and for the experiences I had there.

* * *

I still don't remember a lot on my own. I need pictures and other people to fill in the gaps. My siblings often remind me of how every 6 months we'd drive up to the border of Mexico to renew our tourist visas, living off fruit juice and *plátano manzano* (little "apple bananas" native to Latin America), and visiting the breathtaking tourist town of San Cristóbal de las Casas, Chiapas, on the way.

San Cristóbal was an important hub where indigenous villagers would bring their textiles and food to sell, tourists would walk the streets in shorts and Birkenstock sandals, and migrants would be passing through; we would hear a mix of languages from all over the country and the world. It was a fun and colorful town.

There are moments, impressions and smells that I can recall from Guatemala: its dark, deep green jungles; its awesome white waterfalls; the crazy squawks of colorful parrots and the deep coos of the quetzal birds. I remember hiking and riding my horse and discovering rivers which had boiling water in some parts. I loved Guatemalan food, especially black bean desserts. I loved the feeling of the wet air before and after the rains.

And I remember how my heart would go out to the impoverished indigenous people whom we served. I played with the girls who were our neighbors, and thanks to Facebook, some of us are still friends today. It was there in Guatemala that I learned Spanish. God knew since the beginning of time that I would need, and love, this language, and He made sure I was placed in an area in which I would learn it well and be able to use it in the future for His glory.

It wasn't just my parents doing ministry while we kids did nothing. They also involved me in helping with the children, speaking to them about Jesus, and walking long distances to small villages. I was receiving a firm foundation, being prepared for God to use me to serve in difficult places, to people who had never known positive, nurturing love. It helped me know that a missionary life was not easy - but we were not alone.

I remember reading a passage from the gospel of Matthew, and it stuck with me. Jesus came to his disciples on a mountain and said to them, "All authority has been given to Me in heaven and on earth. Go therefore and make disciples of all the nations, baptizing them in the name of the Father and of the Son and of the Holy Spirit, teaching them to observe all things that I have commanded you; *and lo, I am with you always, even to the end of the age.*"[3] I would read that verse often. It meant a lot to me as a teenager in my active missionary family.

* * *

There is one incident my siblings and I do remember vividly. My older sister was 15 and I was 14, and my parents left us alone with our two younger brothers for the day. My parents were supposed to be back before dark, but they did not quite make it. At that time there was a lot of guerilla and terrorist activity going on in Guatemala. Mom and Dad told us never to open our gate - never to answer anyone who came at night.

But now it was dark, and my parents weren't back yet, and suddenly we clearly heard someone trying to open the gate! The chain rattled and jiggled and the gate banged back and forth, and we were afraid. Whoever it was, they were not giving up.

I told my brothers to stay calm. I grabbed something - I think it was a machete - and opened the front door, telling my brother to shut the door behind me with the latch. As I walked through the front court area towards the gate, I saw my parents' van coming over the hill, their lights shining onto the store in front of us.

At that moment, in the light of the van, I saw two enormous angels with swords in their hands, standing right in front of our home! There is no doubt in my mind what I saw. Did the bad guys see them? I don't know, but in a moment the bad guys were gone, and the angels were still there.

My brothers opened the front door, shouting with both thrill and fear at the sight of the magnificent angels. Then my parents' van approached the gate, and the angels disappeared. We were still trembling as we told Mom and Dad what we'd seen.

---

3. Matthew 28:18-20, NKJV (italics mine)

These types of experiences, as well as the daily devotions and disciplines we had as a family, gave me both stability in my faith and the knowledge that God could do far more than we could ever hope or imagine.

And then, I met Jason.

CHAPTER TWO

I Do

"Put me like a seal over your heart, Like a seal on your arm. For love is as strong as death, Jealousy is as severe as Sheol; Its flashes are flashes of fire, The very flame of the LORD. Many waters cannot quench love, Nor will rivers overflow it; If a man were to give all the riches of his house for love, It would be utterly despised." - Song of Solomon 8:6-7 (NASB)

Marriage was conceived and born in the mind of God.
- Max Lucado

I CAN'T SAY it was love at first sight, but it was pretty close when you think about it. I was only 14 and still living and serving in Guatemala; Jason was almost 17 and on his second mission trip, having already traveled and served in Bolivia. He was tall, blue-eyed, and blond (with a MacGyver mullet), and earnest about serving God. He was from St. Louis, Missouri, finishing high school via homeschool with the Hogans, but his heart was in missions. And it wasn't too long after this that he and his best friend at the time, Joseph Hogan (known to all as Jo-D), began talking seriously about who they were going to marry.

Jason had a girlfriend; but when they began talking about life plans and mission work, it turned out that their directions were not the same. Even as a teenager, Jason could see how important that was, especially for someone who wanted to go 100% into mission work. They called off their relationship.

Since the first time we met, he and I had kept in touch through letters and occasionally seeing each other while I was living in Guatemala, then Mexico, and then Peru, finishing my high school there. At the end of 1990 he was already thinking about me.

We were both in Baton Rouge, Louisiana, with our families for a missions conference at Bethany World Prayer Center, and Jason came to visit me. He gave me a red rose and bought me a black T-shirt: it had a bunch of different types of fish all swimming in one direction and one simply-drawn "Icthus" fish going in the opposite direction, with the words *Go against the flow*. I loved it! And I was flattered to receive Jason's attention, to say the least.

Back in Peru I was invited to be a dorm mother at an orphanage, where children were being rescued from recruitment into a brutal communist guerilla group known as *Sendero Luminoso* (Shining Path) which had ravaged the country. My original plans were to go to nursing school at night while working at the orphanage during the day. But it turned out that I needed a diploma in order to teach at the orphanage, so I ended up returning to Texas, to the language school where my parents had studied, in order to get a degree in Spanish.

It was during my first week at that school, in January 1992, that Jason drove up to Texas from Mexico to see me and take me out on a date. I was unaware but he'd already spoken to my father and asked his permission to marry me, which he'd given. It was a beautifully sunny day. Jason took me to an Italian restaurant and gave me a dozen roses, and asked me to be his wife.

I took a couple of days to give him the answer. *I had to think carefully!* I knew that with Jason as my husband, I'd be staying in a life of full-time missions and service to God. It might be rough and dangerous ... but this was exactly what I felt God was calling me to do. My whole life had been rooted in loving and serving Him. So when I was ready, I gave him my answer. I said "Yes"!

And so began the preparations for a double wedding, with our close friends Jo-D and his fiancé Cindi, who were also planning to go into full-time service with the same mission, Freedom Ministries. I was excited to become the wife of Jason, this awesome, athletic guy whom I admired and loved; I began to imagine all the amazing things we'd do together!

Our double wedding took place in a town called Tamazunchale, in the state of San Luis Potosí, Mexico, on Christmas Eve, December 24, 1992. It was small and beautiful, a wedding based on the style of indigenous Mexican villagers. My dress was white and modestly simple with lace trimmings, and a white and lavender silk ribbon in my hair; and Jason wore blue jeans and a white shirt with a bolo tie. We ate a traditional Mexican wedding meal of chicken *mole* (a combination of chilis and spices mixed as a thick sauce), rice, and Pepsi. Keeping true to cultural tradition in Mexico, Jason didn't smile in any of the pictures.

While Jason's Mom was there and helped us throughout the day, my family couldn't attend. My parents were still in Peru, with my two brothers and baby sister, Hannah. Mom and Dad were involved in several ministries there, in prisons, Bible schools, planting churches, and directing a rehab center. And it was going to cost a lot of money to bring them all up from Peru to Mexico for the wedding. My Mom suggested she could fly up with the baby; but I didn't want them to spend so much money or take out a loan. Jason promised them that we'd meet with them all later, as soon as we could.

The moment we were husband and wife, the moment we said "I do" to each other and before God and those present, we made a covenant that we meant to keep with our whole hearts. Even though I was only 18 and Jason was 20, we knew that our promises were for life, and that we were now a team of two-become-one. We just didn't know how much this commitment would be tested.

* * *

As newlyweds and missionaries, we hit the ground running. From the day we got married, we began living and serving in Mexico, based in a town called Huejutla de Reyes, in the mountains of the state of Hidalgo. Huejutla was - and still is - a hub for the indigenous people from smaller villages to come and sell and buy. In the center of the town there was a massive stone cathedral and convent, built by the Spanish on the foundations of a pyramid designed to worship the Aztec god Tiozihuatl. People in the region dressed in white and spoke Nahuatl, Huasteco and other indigenous languages.

Jason quickly learned phrases in Nahuatl to help him share the gospel, and we made friends in the village who could help translate sermons he wanted to give, so that he could read them aloud and preach in the native language of the people.

From Huejutla we would travel out on bumpy rough dirt tracks to the surrounding villages, past thick green bushes, waterfalls and banana trees. We'd arrive early at a village, Jason would preach the gospel, and I'd gather the children together. We'd sing songs, I'd teach a Bible lesson, give them lollipops, and do arts and crafts with them. We were fervent and so full of energy for Jesus. We loved working together and we loved each other.

Before we got married Jason had purchased a brand new truck for our ministry - a long, green 1992 Dodge Power Ram with a Cummins diesel engine. It had 40-inch tires and loads of ground clearance and was a real beast. It was so strong and necessary for going down the jarring, rocky dirt roads into the isolated villages.

We weren't a perfect couple. We had to learn how to work together both as a couple and as missionaries. But when I think about it, our first year of marriage was filled with joy and fun, a sense of fearlessness, and a growing love for our Lord Jesus and each other. We hardly ever argued. We were both adventurous and up for anything. I was optimistic, friendly, and forgiving, which made me popular among many.

Our love and faith helped us to overcome a very difficult moment in our first year, when I had a miscarriage. It sounds so cold to say it just like that. In reality, having a miscarriage puts an abrupt stop to all the joy and expectation that came before it - and in its place there is a great deal of sadness, emptiness and inner pain. Yet, this affliction drew us closer together, and we trusted in the Lord that He would work all things out for good, because we loved Him and we knew Him to be true to His word.

Over everything, our vision and core values remained the same: *Love God, and help people.*

* * *

In June 1993, six months after our wedding, Jason and I returned to the USA in order to renew our papers. At that time, missionary visas for foreigners had only just been introduced in Mexico, and they were looked upon with a lot of suspicion by Mexican Christian churches and foreign mission societies. Up until then, missionaries would have to go into Mexico as "tourists" for six months at a time. They were then required to leave the country and get a new tourist visa. This is what we still had.

It was the rainy season, and hurricanes were sweeping through the United States, causing massive flooding - this was the year of the catastrophic Great Flood that almost completely wiped out St. Louis. Northern Mexico was also badly hit by floods.

We were on our way to the border, on a deadline to leave Mexico on the very last day of our limited visa. We got to a point about 6 hours from the border of Matamoros and Brownsville when we were forced to stop: the national highway was flooded, with water raging. Thousands of people were stranded, pulled over and waiting in their cars on each side of the road. Then we noticed a semi-trailer and a 1974 Ford F100 attempting to go through the surging water. Watching them from inside our new tough 1-ton diesel truck, Jason was quite sure we could make it as well. And although I was not so sure, we did have to get across the border that day. We pulled out and followed the two vehicles through the water. The people on the side of the road watched us closely.

What an adventure it was, pushing through the water like a bulldozer, feeling the engine working and the tires moving forward even as we went deeper into the strongly moving water. That was, until the semi in front of us lifted up and began to capsize.

I held my breath and we watched it all happen in slow motion. Jason stopped right there in the middle of the river. Water began to seep into our own truck - slowly at first, then filling up the cabin quickly. The semi driver climbed out through his window onto the top of the truck. Jason leaned his head out the window and yelled, "Hold on! We'll come get you!"

The driver looked at the two of us sitting in the rising water inside our green truck, and he signaled to Jason, calling out in Spanish, "Go on ahead. Get your wife to safety, then come back for me."

It was at this point that the water filled up the cabin, higher than the dashboard. Jason tried to put the truck into first ... and the engine on our brand new truck died. We were stranded in the middle of the angry floodwater.

Jason was very strong and I was a lightweight, but he wasn't going to be able to get me to land on his own. A group of 30 or 40 men created a chain, standing firm against the current in order to come and get me; they swung me out of the truck and carried me to safety.

There, at the edge of the bank, we stared at our Dodge. It was going nowhere. We had to wait an entire day until the water went down. We got a tow truck to pull out the truck and drive us up to the Dodge dealership in McAllen, TX where we left the truck for flood repairs and headed back down to Mexico, truckless.

It was disappointing and a little humiliating, not to mention a major setback with respect to our ministry vehicle. Jason felt that as the head of this newly-formed household, he'd made a foolish decision. Thankfully, the vehicle was still under warranty, and the dealership promised us a new engine. We went up to San Antonio for a conference in August, and then returned to McAllen to pick up our truck. But, somehow, it had turned into a giant green lemon. The promised new engine never arrived. Every single week from then on, while we were in Mexico and trying to travel to the villages, something else would break on it.

Early in December 1993, we began the move from our mission base in Huejutla de Reyes to a small indigenous town called Xochiatipan, on the border of the states of Hidalgo and Veracruz. It was nestled in the mountains, a mixture of colorful cement block houses and dark wooden shacks, full of people who'd never heard the gospel of Jesus Christ.

We packed up all our belongings into boxes and bags and dropped them off at our newly built house - so new, it didn't have any interior doors or windows installed yet. We hadn't even slept one night in that little village home, but we had to take a short trip back to the US, for our first all-together family reunion since we'd been married.

I was really excited about this - we both were. We drove our green truck up to Louisiana (thankfully, making it with no problems). My parents and younger siblings flew up from Peru on furlough. My sister Christina, who was living in Italy, flew in for the occasion. Jason's mom also flew down from St. Louis. It was a lot of coordination, but well worth it! We were all together for a wonderful week in Baton Rouge, eating, talking and enjoying the two families - and us, still feeling like newlyweds, almost a year after getting married.

Then it was time to go back to work. We were due at a large conference we'd been helping plan with missionaries from Freedom Ministries in Chiapas, right on the border of Guatemala. We drove down to Victoria, Texas, with my parents and together we attended a church service before saying goodbye.

We were about an hour south of Victoria when the Dodge's transmission gave out completely. Inconvenience was an understatement!

One of the church pastors, John, lent my Dad a vehicle to go get us and take us to a hotel and the truck to the dealership - this time, to the Chrysler workshop. But the question was - how were we going to make it down to Chiapas in time for the conference? We HAD to get there - and we did, by the grace of God. We took a 22-hour bus ride down there, then rode with some friends, and in the back of trucks, and got there in time.

We joined our team and helped at the conference just as we'd planned. Jason rode a bicycle tour with several missionaries that lasted a number of days. And we celebrated our first anniversary while on this trip to Chiapas. We slept on floors here and there in the homes of the missionary families of Freedom

Ministries. It was fun, and beautiful, and we loved being together in the colorful, vibrant town of San Cristóbal de las Casas. Not that I remember any of this. People have told me about it and I've seen the pictures. This is because, one week after celebrating our first anniversary, I died.

CHAPTER THREE

Uprooted

Help me, O Lord my God! Oh, save me according to Your mercy, That they may know that this is Your hand—That You, Lord, have done it! - Psalm 109:26-27 (NKJV)

Trials teach us what we are; they dig up the soil, and let us see what we are made of. – Charles Spurgeon

I T WAS AN unforgettable New Year's Eve, 1993.

The day a large group of armed indigenous guerrillas dressed in army green and balaclavas stormed into San Cristóbal de las Casas - where we'd just stayed - and six other towns in Chiapas in protest of the North American Free Trade Agreement and other changes the Mexican government was making. The Zapatistas, as they called themselves after the revolutionary leader Emiliano Zapata, began a long series of armed combat against the Mexican army "and other repressive forces"[3], setting off bombs in an area of San Cristóbal, right where the other missionary families we'd worked with lived.

The situation was serious and volatile. Anxiously, the missionaries telephoned David Hogan, our leader, who called a meeting with men at the mission base in Raymondville, Texas, to pray and begin organizing an evacuation of the missionaries in coordination with the US Embassy.

The day before, on December 30, after the Chiapas conference, Jason and I had made the long journey back to Texas with some other missionaries to retrieve our poor truck. Brother David Hogan had kindly loaned us his Jeep Cherokee to drive to Victoria and pick it up from the driveway of our friend Pastor John's house.

It was early morning, December 31, and we were in possession of our truck. I drove the Jeep Cherokee; Jason drove our Dodge. We had to return the Jeep to Raymondville, but before going there, we decided to pick up our dog Shadow, a beautiful Rottweiler pup, which we'd left in McAllen before going down to the conference. McAllen was only an hour away from Raymondville, but we went down a different highway to get there. I wasn't familiar with the route, and depended upon Jason to lead the way.

We stopped at a gas station to fill up. Jason walked over to me as I put gas in the Cherokee. "Nicole," he said, "nothing is working in the truck. The flood damaged the whole electrical system. The speedometer is not working. I can't tell how fast I'm going. I could be going 20 miles over the speed limit and I wouldn't know. Why don't you lead and I'll follow you, so we don't get a speeding ticket?"

"Oh J," I replied, "I don't know the way. I don't want to go first. You go first, baby."

I didn't know the way, it's true. But I also believed to my very core that my husband was to be the lead in everything except my relationship with the Lord. I especially didn't want other people to see me leading Jason. I felt it was important for him to go first.

"Don't be stubborn, Nicole. I just want you to be in front so I can judge my speed by your speed."

"I'm not being stubborn. What about if I drive the truck and you drive the Jeep? That way I can follow you and we won't be speeding."

It seemed logical. Jason knew I was confident driving the truck, even with all its problems. So he agreed. Off we went, Jason leading with the cruise control set in the air-conditioned Jeep, listening to Christian music at full volume, and me following in our Dodge that had no gauges working - only the cassette player, with a music tape that a friend had given me, also going at full volume.

It was now bright mid-morning, and we had just driven through Alice, Texas, headed south toward McAllen. It was a straight, flat section of the highway with lanes merging into the highway, a wide median strip down the middle and an unending sky above. Every now and then, Jason would check in the rearview mirror for my green truck following behind. Sometimes I'd see him look and we'd wave and grin at each other.

* * *

December 31, 1993 was also a football Friday, the Vikings vs. the Redskins in an uneasy game for the Redskins. A woman in a house close to the highway was in her kitchen with the TV on the sports channel when she heard the screech of tires out on the highway. She looked out the window, and saw a green truck swerving across all the lanes towards the oncoming traffic on the opposite side, flipping once, twice, three times - on the fourth time she saw a young woman flung out through the windshield and flying through the air! She grabbed her phone and with shaking hands pressed 911 as she kept looking out the window.

"911, what is your emergency?"

"There's a truck out on the road close to where I live. It started flipping. When it flipped the fourth time, I saw a body fly out of the truck," she said with a trembling voice. She glanced out the window again and her eyes widened. "It's STILL FLIPPING! Send help!!" she cried.

***

Jason, still driving along at the speed limit, looked back in the mirror again to check on me, but this time there was no truck behind him. He looked again. Definitely no truck. He glanced in the left mirror to see if I was overtaking him for some reason. I wasn't.

He turned his head to look back, and saw a cloud of dust rising in the air on the median strip and my green truck way over on the opposite side of the highway, past the median and the lanes of oncoming highway traffic. Items from the pickup tray were strewn across the highway. Cars on that side were starting to slow down.

Jason's heart froze. He started praying hard as he looked for a place to do a u-turn. Once he was on the other side of the highway and at the place where the truck stood he parked the Jeep close by and got out fast. The truck had landed upright, but the roof of the truck on the left side had caved in and the windshield and windows were gone. The left door and front of the vehicle were just twisted pieces of metal. The entire truck was crumpled like a piece of paper thrown into the trash. Jason could hear the stereo speakers still blaring a song by Wes King through the cabin's open spaces.

He looked for me inside the cabin, but I wasn't in there. Another man hurried past him towards the grass at the fence line. It was a fair distance from the right side of the truck, over 90 feet (30m) away. Jason followed him over there, and that was when he saw my body on the ground.

I was unconscious, lying face down, my arms at a strange

angle behind my back and my hands at my shoulders. Jason first thought that all my arms and legs were broken. Then he saw my face turned to the side. There was blood, so much blood, coming from my eyes, nose and ears. He heard gasping, gurgling sounds from my throat - then silence. The man who had reached me first was kneeling next to me. He turned to Jason; Jason noticed the man was of Asian descent.

"I doctor," he said soberly. "She going to die. The injuries are too great." Moments later he checked my pulse. "No need to call physician. She dead."

Jason's knees gave out and he fell to the ground. His mind refused to work properly. Wasn't he just driving down the road in that great little Jeep Cherokee? Didn't he just celebrate his first anniversary in Mexico with his young, healthy, spirited wife? What was this? What was happening?

The other bystanders coming to see the wreck saw a young man collapse near the fallen, bloodied young woman. They thought he'd just been driving down the highway, and like them, had come to see what had happened, not prepared for the injuries he saw. They helped him up; but no one realized he was my husband.

Sirens announced the arrival of the police with an ambulance; the paramedics assessed the situation quickly without touching me, and called for a HALO emergency helicopter. Just before the helicopter arrived, they began to prep me so that the HALO team could properly treat the most urgent injuries. They began to cut off my bloodied clothing, including the beautiful hiking boots I'd just purchased. When Jason saw them, he mentioned to one of the paramedics that I'd be upset about those hiking boots getting destroyed. It was a crazy thing to say, but it was all his mind could focus on. He was in shock.

The paramedics assumed I was unmarried and alone, and didn't ask anyone. They loaded me carefully into the helicopter and it rose up and flew away.

Jason was still in a daze when he saw the helicopter take off. He approached one of the police officers. "Hey, where are they taking her?"

The police officer didn't want to give any information away to a stranger until Jason told him, "I'm her husband. I need to know where she's going."

"What happened here?" the police officer asked him.

"I dunno. Maybe she was adjusting the stereo or something. I can't think what happened." Jason shook his head in confusion.

The police officer finally told him the helicopter would be taking me to Memorial Medical Center in Corpus Christi, roughly 50 miles (85 km) away. Jason climbed into the Jeep, focused only on getting to the hospital as fast as he could. But when he arrived, found the Emergency Room and approached the front desk, he had no idea what to do or say.

"Nicole Fitzpatrick," he said to the medical staff. "She's my wife. She's 19 years old. She had an accident. I don't know how it happened."

The receptionist looked up the list of names of newcomers. "There's no Nicole Fitzpatrick here, sir," she replied. She looked more carefully at the sheet in front of her. "There's ... there's a Jane Doe here. She came in a little while ago by the HALO emergency team. She's in the ICU."

"That's her!" said Jason. "She came in by helicopter. Her name is Nicole Fitzpatrick. We're married. I'm her husband." But he had no way to prove it. He didn't know what else to do or say. He sat down in a hard red plastic chair, feeling blank, useless and utterly miserable.

The ER nurse found my driver's license - it still had my maiden name on it, Angela Nicole Mason. We'd gotten married and begun ministering immediately in Mexico; I hadn't had time - or made time - to make changes to any of my official documents. The nurse located details for an emergency contact on my license, and rang Freedom Ministries. Debbie Hogan, David's wife, took the phone call. Debbie confirmed that she knew Angela Mason. She asked to speak to Jason.

"Jason, what happened? Are you okay? How is Nicole?" she asked.

Jason's shocked mind began to fuddle all the details. "We were driving to get gas. I was driving the Dodge. No, the Jeep. Nicole was driving the Jeep. No, wait ... I can't remember. The truck ... They cut up her brand new boots! She's bleeding everywhere. I don't think she's got any teeth left! I don't know what's going on, Mrs Debbie. I don't know if she's alive or - or not. They won't tell me anything 'cause I can't prove we're married."

Debbie reassured him that they'd get there as soon as they could, then asked to speak to someone from Intensive Care.

"The Jane Doe in ICU," Debbie said to them carefully, "is Angela Nicole Fitzpatrick. Her maiden name is Mason. I promise you it's her. Look on the top of her left arm; there's a scar from a dog bite. The young man outside is Jason Fitzpatrick; he is Nicole's husband. Please keep informing him of her condition. We'll try to get there as soon as possible."

"Ma'am, where are you coming from?" the ICU nurse asked.

"We're in Raymondville," replied Debbie.

"Even if you left right now, Ma'am, I'm afraid you won't make it in time. Mrs Fitzpatrick will have passed away before you arrive. I'm very sorry."

Debbie hung up the phone and rushed to tell David, who was still in the meeting with the other men, working through the procedures to evacuate the missionaries from San Cristóbal and praying for the conflict in Chiapas. Mrs Debbie wouldn't normally interrupt a meeting like this, but this was too important to follow protocol. Jason was their spiritual son, and his wife was about to die.

They contacted Britt and Audrey Hancock, the Freedom Ministries prayer team directors, who began to organize intercession for me and my family. Hundreds of people across the nation began to pray. Then the Hogans left immediately for Corpus Christi, bringing three other friends: Jay and Judy Williams, and Greg Rider, a fellow missionary and close family friend.

When they arrived in the late afternoon, the ER waiting room was full; they found Jason sitting silently against the wall, his hoodie covering his head. He was still unable to act, or speak. His hands were cold. David, Debbie, and Judy went to find the doctors and ask about my condition, leaving Jason in the waiting room with Greg and Jay. Judy was a registered nurse, so she was permitted to go into ICU.

A little later, Dr. Mark Geneser, the pulmonologist, came into the waiting room. He had kind eyes, but his face was grim - and he was covered in blood. "I need the husband to come with me into the operating room right now," he said. Jason looked up, and was helped to his feet by David and Greg. He walked into the ICU with Debbie, David and Judy by his side, and saw me, his once vibrant wife, still and silent on the operating table.

The sheets were full of blood. There were many machines making noise around me and tubes attached to me. My entire chest was open, right down to my lower abdomen. Several ribs were broken. Jason took all this in at once, and fainted.

"Wake him up, quickly," said the doctor. The nurses began working at bringing Jason back to consciousness. The doctor began his assessment. "Both her lungs collapsed and her internal organs have all been severely damaged. She has significant head trauma with a cerebral contusion. She has many broken ribs and vertebrae. She was basically dead on arrival, but somehow she's still with us. The good thing is that her bleeding has stopped, so we won't have to do heart surgery. However, I'm afraid she has little chance of survival. We are going to do emergency surgery right now.

"This is Dr. Susan Douglas, the anesthesiologist. We also have here Dr. Paul Zanetti, our neurologist, and Dr. William Sheffield, orthopedic surgeon. Mr. Fitzpatrick, as her husband, we'll need you to sign a number of consent forms and legal documents on her behalf. We also need you to answer some health questions for us."

Jason was forced to make some important decisions for me, even in his state of shock. As the husband he had to be in charge of what was going to happen with me. It was a difficult responsibility for a 21-year old, but he did it.

Debbie could see that my survival depended only on the Lord's mercy, and that God's peace and comfort were required. She spoke up. "Dr. Geneser, can we please pray for her?"

The doctors all assented, even though at least one of them didn't believe God existed. None of them imagined I would actually survive what I had gone through. They were all expecting the worst, and had already informed Jason and all the family and friends to do the same. Certainly the power for me to live was not in their hands. Still, they removed their head coverings respectfully and bowed their heads.

Debbie went to the end of the bed, and gently took my feet in her hands. The group pleaded for the blood of Jesus to cover me and heal me. They prayed for the doctors who would be operating on me, and for the Father's name to be glorified. Then they said "Amen", took one last look at me, and left the room.

My parents were not together when they heard the news. My Dad was attending an Annual General Meeting in Mississippi, and Mom was shopping with her parents and siblings at a Walmart in Ville Platte, near Baton Rouge. She heard her name called over the intercom as she was checking out. Her cousin's wife told her about the wreck and she left immediately with her younger sister, my dear Aunt Michelle, driving straight to Baton Rouge where she met up with my Daddy.

Since it was New Year's Eve, all the flights were full. No-one was willing to miss their flight ... until a kind elderly couple gave up their seats for my parents to see their daughter. They made it to the hospital in Corpus Christi at around midnight, along with Aunt Michelle.

They met with Jason and the others in the ICU waiting room. It was a quiet, tense reunion filled with unknowns and uncertainties, yet also with much prayer. My Mom and Dad were allowed in to see me, for what they thought would be the last time. Mom was not at all prepared for what she saw. As she walked back into the waiting room, she leaned her back against the wall and slid down to the floor, devastated.

Many hours later, Dr. Geneser came out with the news - "She made it through the surgery. She's stable for the moment. We'll have to do a lot more operations in the future, and we can't promise anything, but right now she's still holding on!"

My family and friends erupted into praise and thanks to the almighty God and His awesome power to save me from death. It truly was a testimony to the reality of God, especially for the doctor who had not believed that God even existed. What we didn't know was that even earlier than this, others had been praying for me.

CHAPTER FOUR

Not Alone

The LORD *has heard my supplication; The* LORD *will receive my prayer. - Psalm 6:9 (NKJV)*

Prayer is the exercise of drawing on the grace of God. - Oswald Chambers

I THANK THE Lord that this accident occurred in South Texas, where just a few years earlier, some concerned citizens had seen the need for emergency services to get critically injured people to a hospital more quickly than in an ambulance. They created a non-profit charity called HALO-Flight Inc. and began offering the air-rescue service to anyone in need, regardless of their ability to pay.[4] The helicopter arrived within minutes of my accident and the 911 call.

My mother-in-law was very upset that no-one in the local law enforcement had thought to ask if there were any family members present at the wreck. Thus, Jason was not with me inside the helicopter. Yet, I was not alone - my heavenly Father was by my side throughout the flight. This is obvious, because

I died several times on the flight, and each time He brought me back to life.

A few years after my time in the hospital, I had the opportunity to speak on the phone to one of the medical staff from HALO to find out more about the flight and to thank them for what they did for me. The rescue attendant could hardly believe his ears when I told him who I was.

"Wow, you made it through?!" he exclaimed. "I'm one of the guys who picked you up! I was on that flight! I remember you! I can't believe this - you really made it!"

He was very enthusiastic to be able to speak to me about that flight to Memorial Medical Center. "We all thought you weren't going to make it. We were doing our very best, but your heart stopped beating several times on that flight. Each time we tried to shock you to bring you back, you didn't respond. So we'd look at the clock and announce the time of death and get ready to write it down, and then all of a sudden your mouth would open and you'd draw in breath. It was so amazing!"

I felt privileged that God had led me to this particular man who could give me all the details of what happened that day.

"We could see that one lung had collapsed and you were barely pulling any oxygen into the other lung. It kept going like this, you'd stop breathing and we thought you were dead, and then suddenly you'd take another breath. We shocked you back five times on that flight! When we landed on the roof of the hospital in Corpus Christi, both your lungs collapsed. But then the hospital staff took over from us. We honestly didn't think you'd make it."

I shared with the rescue attendant that I was a Christian, and knew that God had been with me during this horrific ordeal and had allowed me to survive. Incredibly, he got even more excited.

"You know, after we dropped you off, we all went back to the

HALO base, and we told all the other guys there of how badly you were injured and what had happened on the flight, the way you kept dying and coming back. And do you know what we did? We all joined hands and prayed for you!"

What a great God we have! He hears and answers prayer!

CHAPTER FIVE

Trust and Obey

I will lift up the cup of salvation, And call upon the name of the LORD. - Psalm 116:13 (NASB)

Lord ... help me to keep all of my dreams on Your altar and be ready at all times to respond with faith and obedience to Your call. – Colin S. Smith

THE FIVE MAIN doctors assigned to my case had very little hope for me surviving much into the New Year of 1994. I was in an induced coma and on life support, with a tracheostomy tube in my throat to help me breathe. I had a very long pin secured to my skull to reduce pressure and swelling on one side, and my head was surrounded by metal bars to hold it in place and to allow healing of the vertebrae. The doctors considered that if I did survive I'd be brain-dead, unable to move or do anything at all.

This was terrible news for Jason. He was stoic, showing great patience and endurance throughout this entire ordeal. But he was also often totally overwhelmed by the negativity and discouragement. It was difficult to go to the ICU every day for 6 weeks and see tragedy and pain and distraught family members. An atmosphere of tension and misery was constant. Not a day went past when somebody didn't pass away. It was depressing, and scary. Jason understandably developed a deep dislike for hospitals, making him nauseous from anxiety.

There were times when Jason just had to get away from the ICU, away from the drama and the tears. He discovered the hospital's chapel, and found solitude there. It was a small, simply decorated place that served all denominations; one area was for Catholics, another for Protestants.

He was often able to sit alone in that calm place, just to pray to God and think and ponder. What would life be like for him if I didn't survive? And what would it be like if I did? He loved the Lord, and wanted to be a willing vessel in His hands. But he didn't understand anything that was going on, or why.

One day, while I was still in a coma, Jason was sitting in the chapel, silently praying, when he heard the doors open behind him. A man pushed his way through the doors in a wheelchair. He was attached to a number of machines with tubes; as he moved, he pulled them along with him, until he stopped in front of one of the Catholic statues. He began to cry and tremble, praying in Spanish. All he could say was "*Dios, ¿por qué?*" ("God, why?")

Jason had never seen this man or met him before, but he could tell that he was praying as best he knew how. Jason tried to continue in his own prayers, but he couldn't. He felt the Holy Spirit say, "Get up and go minister to him."

This was tough. Jason was still feeling down, and tried to fight the Holy Spirit's prompting, justifying himself in his conscience. "No. No! I'm going through my own stuff. My wife's in a coma. I don't want to go and minister. I don't want to be a minister right now."

But then he remembered the scripture from 2 Timothy: "Preach the word; be ready *in season and out of season* ..."[4] In his heart of hearts, Jason knew that he still served God first, despite everything that was going on in his life and with his wife. So, in obedience, he got up and sat down close to the distraught man. He said, "Hey, man, you know ... you look pretty bad off. I'm sorry. ..."

The man looked at Jason, and introduced himself as Saul. He began to share his situation with Jason, thankful for an ear willing to listen. He had several diseases and problems; but his main issue was that he was dying from tuberculosis. He'd had blood transfusions and was taking countless medicines. His lungs were collapsing, he was on a breathing machine, and he was dying. Saul was indeed pretty bad off.

Jason realized two things: that this man needed Jesus, and that he was still the Lord's servant, to seek and to save in Jesus' name those who are lost - even in the Memorial Medical Center chapel. As he began to speak, Jason understood that the Lord was helping him look past his own difficulties and speak life into the soul of someone who was about to die and spend eternity in Hell.

"You know, I'm sorry you feel like this and that you're going through this, but I need to tell you, it's appointed to us all to die once and then after that is the judgment day. And you know, I can pray that God heals you, and I believe that He can. But more than anything, you need to get your soul right with Jesus. You need to repent, and be born again."

Saul looked at Jason curiously. "You sound just like John Osteen," he said to Jason.

This was January 1994. Long before Joel Osteen came on the scene, his father, John Osteen, had been a strong hell-fire-and-brimstone gospel preacher who would call all who

---

4. 2 Timothy 4:2, NASB (italics mine)

heard to repent and get on their knees and cry out to Jesus for salvation. Saul had listened to John preach on a TV in the ICU. "That's what John Osteen said. We got to be born again. I want to ... but I don't know how."

Jason sensed that God was speaking to Saul to bring Him to salvation. He led Saul to pray and ask God to save him. Saul repented of his sins and gave his life to Jesus in that little chapel. Jason laid hands on Saul and prayed for him - for peace, life, and healing. There were tears. In truth, they were ministering to each other. When they said goodbye, Saul told him which room he was in, and Jason said he'd look for him.

The next few days, Jason would visit Saul in his hospital room and pray for him as he lay in bed hooked up to the machines. With all the tension and uncertainty of seeing me lying in a coma, these joyful encounters were profoundly encouraging moments for Jason - until a few days later he went into Saul's room and found it completely empty. All Saul's things were gone, the machines had been removed, and the bed was empty. The afternoon sun was pouring into the quiet room. Jason's first sinking thought was, "He's dead. He passed away."

He sat in the visitor's chair for a few minutes and thought about things. He thought about me. I was still in a coma, still in a critical state. The hospital staff were still of the opinion that I would not survive. Yet Jason had kept ministering to Saul, bringing him to salvation and to joy in his new faith in God. *At least now*, he thought, *he's rejoicing in heaven.*

Jason noticed a nurse walking past Saul's room. He called out to her, "Hey, what happened to the patient that was here, Saul?"

She answered, "Well, we ran tests yesterday, and last night, and again this morning. He came back totally negative for everything. He's perfectly fine. He could walk and breathe. So we let him go. He's gone home! It was amazing," she added with a light in her eyes. "It was like a miracle happened to him."

Jason left Saul's room, and began the route back to mine, walking faster and faster. He wanted to leap in the air, he felt so encouraged! He told my Mom and my brother Lucas. It was a special moment. God saved and healed Saul!

A couple of days later, Saul came back to the hospital to see Jason. This turned into a regular thing. He'd come to sit with me in the ICU; then he and Jason would go and have coffee and talk about the Lord and about Saul's life. Saul had lots of questions.

"What do I do, man? I used to deal drugs and make a load of money. And now my wife is mad at me because now I'm a Christian and I can't go back to that lifestyle. I'm never going to go back. What should I do?"

Jason looked at him and said, "I'm not going to tell you what to do. I think in your heart you know what you have to do." It was Saul's job to seek the face of the Lord and discover His will.

"My whole life is changing," Saul continued. "I can't stop reading the Bible and listening to John Osteen."

Sure enough, Saul told his wife he was going to serve God, get a job, and never go back to his old life. He flushed all his drugs down the commode. God healed him completely and gave him a new life in Christ. And He used Jason to reach him, even in Jason's weakness and personal pain.

I would never say that God made me have a horrendous accident for this purpose. But "God causes all things to work together for good to those who love God, to those who are called according to His purpose."[5] I clung on to this verse as my lifeline for many years. And it's obvious that He had more in store for me.

---

5. Romans 8:28, NASB

Chapter Six

Uncertain Times

Rejoice with those who rejoice, and weep with those who weep. - Romans 12:15 (NASB)

In perplexities – when we cannot tell what to do, when we cannot understand what is going on around us – let us be calmed and steadied and made patient by the thought that what is hidden from us is not hidden from Him. - Frances Ridley Havergal

FOR THE FIRST 11 days of January, I was completely comatose. Then I opened my eyes. The medical staff kept me under sedation in the ICU for just over a month after that. It was during this time that I'd wake up occasionally, disconcerted and confused, unable to recognize anyone or remember anything. It was a tough time for all my family - everyone had to adjust to this new, emotionally demanding situation. They never knew how I would react when I awoke. Yet God was still in control.

Jason and my parents met a Christian couple who were visiting the ICU to pray for a patient. Fernando and Cindy Trujillo owned a small, one-bedroom beach house in an area called the

Rock Lodge in Corpus Christi, and they allowed my family to stay there for free the entire time I was in the hospital. What an amazing blessing! People gave so generously to us during this time! (And it has been a friendship for life.)

I wasn't able to hear much or comprehend, but I received a lot of spiritual input during those days. My Dad would read the Bible to me for hours throughout the day, every day for two months, in English and Spanish. Every Friday (and sometimes even more frequently) while in the ICU, a woman from our home church in Louisiana would drive to Corpus Christi in order to sit in my room, play her guitar and sing praise and worship songs. I didn't even know who she was - yet she had such compassion to simply come and sit and worship the Lord by my bedside.

Our friends and prayer warriors, Britt and Audrey Hancock, were instrumental in coordinating ongoing prayer for me during these months. They also came to visit and care for us. Britt sat with Jason in the small ICU waiting room, and their small daughter Hannah climbed up into Jason's lap. He held her for a long time. Audrey came in to see me, with my "halo pins" stuck in my head to keep me still and prevent more brain swelling. She sat and prayed for me, and gently painted my fingernails red so that I'd feel pretty when I woke up.

Other friends of mine would come in and sing worship songs. Hundreds of unknown people came to the hospital to see me! They drove from all over the USA! Some even flew in to see me - and that's back in 1994 when flights were expensive. Missionaries all around the world were praying for me; some came to visit me. Many who came were people I'd met or talked to at some point in my early years. In some small way I had touched their lives, and now they were coming to touch mine. God sent them to pray for me and to love me and my family. My best friends Jena Wesley, Penny McGee, Donna Alford, and

Jayne Brown were constantly there for me. Jena called me every single day for an entire year.

It affected me greatly that such an outpouring of love would be shown to me in that hospital room. It continues to affect me. It is precious, and special; a sign of the Body of Christ made real through practical actions of love and care. And of course my husband, my parents and my siblings were there, praying faithfully for me. A number of the medical staff around me also had a degree of trust in the Lord for my life.

Jason and my parents would come early every day to spend the day with me. Then, in the early afternoon, they would all go back to the Trujillos' little beach house. Jason would take a shower, eat a meal with my parents, and then come back to the hospital. Sometimes, he'd sleep in the waiting room, or sit by my bed all night, or curl up on the floor in my room. None of them had any idea what my future would look like. They just took it faithfully, each day, for one more day.

Whenever I woke up, my family would talk to me and patiently tell me who I was, who they were, and why I was there. Sometimes I would recognize Mama. At first I didn't recognize Jason at all; on some days I thought he was a doctor or nurse, on others the pizza delivery boy; and often I would just be terribly confused and utterly dependent on the adults around me.

It didn't help that a few well-meaning people would come in and try to explain what had happened to me based on their own ideas or understanding of theology. Sometimes their words were cruel. Back in the 90's, the consensus among many Christians in the US concerning mental illness and brain injury was, "Oh, she's gone crazy. It's an attack from Satan. Nicole's being spiritually blocked. She needs to be delivered and get set free from those demons in her, and then she'll remember everything again!"

Thankfully, the neurologist and nurses sat down with my

family and explained to them what was actually happening to me, to help them understand better what I was going through and what was required of them.

"Nicole has significant brain damage. It's known as Traumatic Brain Injury, or TBI", said the neurologist, Dr. Zanetti. "She is also showing symptoms of Post-Traumatic Amnesia. The parts of her brain that deal with learning and remembering have been damaged from the accident. It's very common for people with TBI to have memory problems. At present, she can't remember anything about the incident that caused the injury. There are some things she might never remember."

"She might never remember who I am?" asked Jason, stricken.

"That is a possibility you'll have to consider. TBI can affect both short-term and long-term memory. People with TBI may have a tough time "remembering to remember" things they have to do in the future, such as keeping appointments or calling someone back. But there are certain strategies that can help people with TBI to learn to work around memory problems and start to function better each day. We'll help you with those. You might well find that if she survives and recovers and she continues with rehabilitation, Nicole's memory will start to improve over time." *If she survives.* This was the daily uncertainty my family faced.

At this early point, whenever I woke up, after recovering from the shock of thinking I was in the 4077th Mobile Hospital with Hawkeye and Klinger - the characters from *M*A*S*H* - I would be unable to take in what people were telling me. I refused to believe I was married. My brain had regressed to the state of a pre-adolescent. I'd tell anyone who'd listen, "I'm not married; I'm still in school!" Not even this made sense, because I couldn't remember anything about school.

But it went deeper than just my memory; I had a type of

aphasia, being able to say words and phrases, but not knowing what they meant. I didn't know what questions to ask that could bring me any level of understanding, either. I felt totally lost, disoriented, and nauseous from the bed that kept slowly moving. Thank God He surrounded me with my patient, loving family and the hospital staff around me.

At one point, in my confused state, I decided I needed to get out of bed. I had to be free. Off to one side I saw a dark hallway and a light; I felt the need to walk towards that light. I pulled out as many tubes as I could from my body, swung my feet round towards the floor and actually stood up for a few seconds. There was a young nurse standing nearby - she gasped and dropped all the papers she was holding, just as I fell to the floor in a pool of blood. I don't remember getting helped carefully back into bed, or having the tubes reattached. But I know that those tubes sticking into me added to my sense of being held a prisoner against my will.

Jason was so relieved when I was finally released from the ICU, six weeks later, away from the atmosphere of trauma and death ... but the road was still a hard one. First, I was transferred to the 4th floor for major, all-day-long surgeries on the vertebrae in my back and almost every internal organ; following those grueling surgeries, I was placed in a full body brace. I had pain in my head, throat, chest, abdomen, back, and hip, where they'd taken bone to create new vertebrae. Three weeks after this, I was moved up to the Rehab center on the 8th floor for therapy.

It was in late February, my last days on the 4th floor, that I first recognized my brother Lucas. When Jason alerted the medical staff, they called Dr. Zanetti, the neurologist, to come and assess me. He began to ask me a series of questions.

"Let's see how much you're able to remember, Nicole. Who was President of the United States when you were born?"

I had no idea. My mind drew a complete blank. He might as well have asked me to point out the New Hebrides on a map. In fact, I failed every single one of the questions he asked me. It was still in the early days. But recognizing Lucas was a start, and it gave everyone hope that I might slowly recover.

At every stage, the doctors continued to predict that I would not survive, or be able to walk again. But each week God brought about more recovery. It was not easy ... there was nothing easy about any moment of any of these days. Every day was a battle, and felt like a thousand years. But God was there. And there were two things I never lost. One was the knowledge that God was real and loved me. And the other was my ability to speak Spanish.

There was a Latin American nurse in the hospital who helped me after my surgeries. She was small in stature and had long hair that, when let down, went past her waist. When it was her shift to care for me, I would call her "Nanny" and speak Spanish to her. To all the other nurses I spoke English. It seems that somehow my brain connected her with my Godmother from childhood, who was French, small in stature and had hair down to her ankles. I hardly remember my French Nanny, except that she too was a nurse, had a sweet smile and wore cowboy boots.

Yet this Latina nurse reminded me so much of my French Nanny, that subconsciously I thought she was the same person - yet spoke to her not in French but in Spanish. I am so thankful that my Mama was there to help me figure out these strange connections I was making as I recovered. For Dr. Zanetti, the neurologist, this was a good sign; it showed that my brain was working, putting things together, even though it was in a weird way.

* * *

Once I moved to the rehab unit, I was given eight daily sessions of therapy, with some therapies repeated more than once during the day: speech, occupational, psychological, physical, respiratory, and reading therapy. I was like a small child; I had to learn to do everything again. It took me 10 minutes to walk just a few feet. I had to practice using my voice to speak after they removed the tracheostomy tube. I didn't know how to hold a pen or write anything; I could only scribble.

The therapy was very methodical work - a regimen designed to help me take one step at a time while bringing structure and order into my life. I ate at this hour; I went to the bathroom at that hour. I showered at this time. At the time, I hated it. Everything was so difficult. I felt like a prisoner because of this strict schedule. This too contributed to my ongoing confusion about being in some kind of prison camp.

And yet, even during this stage when my mind was a fog and I hardly knew anyone, I knew phone numbers from the past. I couldn't match the numbers with names, but I could rattle off the combinations in my head. Except for my Grandma Charlie's number - I could remember the number, and that it was hers. One day I asked my Mom to pass me the phone.

"I'm going to call Grandma," I said.

"*Grandma*? You can't possibly know Grandma's number!" she replied, narrowing her eyes in disbelief.

"Yes, I do," I answered her. "It's 318-363-5768." And I dialed it.

My Mom was amazed. "Nicole, you don't even know who *we* are - and you know Grandma's number?"

"Hello, Grandma?" I said to the phone.

Mom would also talk about this with Dr. Zanetti. "I don't understand how she can remember numbers and not her own family."

"Was she good at Math?" asked the neurologist.

"She aced it. She was always good at Algebra."

"Well, that's the strong part of her brain. She's a numbers person," he replied. "Her brain is starting to respond to the connections that are strongest for her."

My memory also slowly started coming back through dreams. It was not as if I could suddenly remember something new; but I'd have a dream about an event or experience that had occurred in my life. At times the memories were mixed up. Things were still terribly confusing for me. There were times when Jason thought I was going crazy and would say so; sometimes I thought I was going crazy, too. For all intents and purposes, I guess I was a little crazy during that time. It'd be quite a while before I could truly say I was "thinking straight".

And for a time, things continued to go downhill.

CHAPTER SEVEN

Who Am I?

"Listen! My beloved! Behold, he is coming, leaping on the mountains, jumping on the hills!" - Song of Solomon 2:8 (NASB)

Turn full your soul's vision to Jesus, and look and look at Him, and a strange dimness will come over all that is apart from Him. - Lilias Trotter[6]

I HAD A lot of visitors. Apart from regular visits from friends and family, people from far away would also come to see me. Although the visitors meant well and some were very comforting, quite often they tired me more than encouraged me.

Total strangers (to me) would come in and say cheerily, "Hi Nicole, remember me?" I'd look at them blankly and shake my head. "Oh come on!" they'd go on with a smile. "Of course you do! Don't you remember that we used to ..." - and they'd tell me something we apparently often did together. Nothing rang any

---

6. This quote from Lilias Trotter, missionary to Algeria, became the inspiration for the beloved hymn "Turn Your Eyes Upon Jesus".

bells. "Come on, surely you must remember the time when you came to my house and ..."

After a while their insistence that I remembered them began to irritate me. They wouldn't accept my "no" as a real or legitimate answer. It was as if I had to perform for them, so that they wouldn't feel hurt that I couldn't remember anything about them. I learned that it was a lot easier to simply nod and pretend I knew who they were. But that also got me into trouble, especially the next time they came to visit and I gave them the blank look again. "Now don't tell me you don't remember, Nicole! We've been through this before. You *do* remember and you know it!"

People would say unhelpful, thoughtless things as well, such as, "You must be so happy just to be alive!" or "I had a friend who was in a car accident once, but he died", or "So exactly what caused the wreck? Was it your fault?" or "Have you tried asking for God's forgiveness?"

I didn't remember any part of the accident. I didn't remember if I'd done something that might have caused the wreck to happen. It left an unanswerable puzzle in my mind. I did a lot of crying.

There was a moment when all my therapists had a meeting with my Mom and me. There were about 7 or 8 specialists together in the room, discussing my progress in front of me. It was tough. I don't remember much about this meeting until the occupational therapist, in charge of helping me relearn to do simple daily chores and activities, spoke up, and said something I will never forget.

"I think she's faking a lot of this. I think she just wants attention."

At the time and in the state I was in, I wasn't able to respond. Thankfully, others did. The physical therapist - a kind Filipina - defended me and tried to say something less hurtful - although it did still hurt. "I think she's trying to do her best. I know she's got it in her to get better. But I suspect she's just not putting in enough effort, quite yet."

It was the speech therapist who spoke up on my behalf, in his deep southern Mississippi accent. "Well, I think she's doing the very best she can. I don't think she's faking at all. She's made some great progress and I know she'll keep improving."

It truly is amazing to note the difference between receiving words of encouragement that speak positively towards the future, and hearing negative and hurtful opinions all the time. One allows you to look forward and have hope and find purpose; the other, to consider how much you've lost, making you believe you'll never do anything again, no matter how hard you try, because your current reality defines who you are and who you'll always be.

One of the strategies the neurologist encouraged my Mom to do was to put up pictures on the walls, pictures of me growing up with my friends and loved ones. She stuck up as many pictures as she could, in the hopes that it would jog my memories. It was a useful thing to do, and it did help, but it was also hurtful in a way none of us could have imagined.

For those months that I was on the 4th floor and in the rehab unit, hundreds of people - doctors, nurses, interns, attorneys, local Christians - would come into my room and see the pictures on the walls - especially a large framed photograph next to my bed which showed me in a long, pretty graduation dress. And they would say, "Wow, she is beautiful! Who is that? Is that your sister? You have the same eyes!" They would wonder who that pretty girl was - and not see that it was *me*! The family member who was with me at the time would explain that it was me in the picture.

Sometimes I was able to tell them myself. "That was me, two years ago", I'd say. And the embarrassed flush would creep into their face - especially the male nurses, pastors, and doctors! I remember the respiratory therapist who was giving me exercises to learn how to breathe on my own again without the trach tube. He was keen to find out who the picture of the beautiful girl was - and so embarrassed when he discovered it was me. He quickly apologized and told me I still looked beautiful.

But this daily experience hurt me a great deal - especially because sometimes people would respond with, "Well, that *was* Nicole!" Then they'd proceed to tell me who I once *was*.

"You were always a happy, chipper type of girl."

"Nicole, you were always the life of the party."

"You were the fun one. Man, you were such a clown! You'd make everyone laugh."

"Wow, Nicole, you used to be fearless. You were ready to try anything."

Even Jason would do it. I understand now that he was young, struggling with his own process of grieving and trying to come to terms with life as it was right then, but it was hard to hear at the time. "You were the best wife ever! You were so in love with Jesus. You were so beautiful, and industrious, and hard working! But you'll never be that again! It's all gone now."

These were all the things the people who'd known me before would tell me I *was*. But I didn't feel like I was that girl anymore. And the truth is, I didn't *look* anything like the girl in the picture anymore.

Before the accident, I was small and fit, weighing about 110lb (about 50kg). During my time in the ICU, the feeding tube to my stomach allowed my weight to stay about the same. But when I went to rehab, they removed the tubes to my stomach and throat, putting me on soft, solid food again. The problem was, I couldn't eat - I began throwing up everything. I kept nothing down. I lost a lot of weight very quickly. I went all the way down to 80lb (36kg), my eyes looked disproportionately large and dark, my face and body were as thin as a rake, and my skin was a pasty white.

A different battle began to rage within me. I started to feel tired, lost, and desperate. I was tired of feeling like I was always being interrogated by the doctors, answering the same questions over and over. Tired of waking up confused and disoriented and not knowing who these people were who were calling themselves my family and friends. Tired of the constant effort of thinking, of working at my rehabilitation, of trying to please all the therapists. Tired of hearing people telling me I must be just so happy to be alive. Tired of others saying to me, "You were ..." and "You used to ...".

If the girl in that photograph was Nicole, then who was I?

There is a picture that was taken of me in my hospital bed at about this time. My brothers and my younger sister Hannah were visiting with my Mom. In the picture, Hannah is sitting on my Mom's lap. They must have brought me a plush toy because I'm holding one with the tag still on it. Everyone looks active and happy and bright - except for me, lying on my side on the bed, turned away from my family, with expressionless eyes, looking immensely lost. I have no ability or desire to even look at the person taking the picture. I am depressed, and I am suffering.

* * *

There was a day when a nurse wheeled a cart into my room and set it beside my bed. I saw it had a number of other patients' pills in little cups on the top tier. I don't know what confusing thought occurred to me at that moment. I was at rock bottom. I wasn't getting better. I felt so tired of everything.

As the nurse turned away from me to write something down, I reached for the little cups and started dashing the pills into my mouth. The nurse caught me, pulled the cart away from me, and immediately shouted for assistance.

"Help me! We've got to pump her stomach! She took all those pills! I don't know how many cups she grabbed!"

The nurse got into trouble for leaving the cart within my reach. And I got into trouble too: they tied me to the bed again.

Months before, I'd been restrained in a special oscillating bed that moved in order to avoid bedsores. But now I was in rehab and supposed to be slowly moving again; except that now my arms were held down with white material. I wasn't being tortured - but I did feel like a proper prisoner, and it was so very hard for me. I cried a lot, especially when I was on my own. And I began to question God.

"Why, God? Was this all my fault? Am I supposed to be dead? I'm causing a lot of suffering. Why am I still here? Why can't I remember anything? Why can't I remember anyone, God?"

One afternoon soon after this incident I was alone, feeling exhausted, and silently crying, my tears running down my cheeks, into my ears and wetting my braided hair and pillow. "I can't do this, God!" I prayed in desperation. "Please show me what You expect from me! Why did this happen? Who am I, Lord?"

I didn't want to live; I didn't want to die.

I drifted towards sleep.

* * *

Maybe what happened next was a dream. Maybe it was a vision. Whatever it was, while I lay in my hospital bed, God allowed me to remember the truck and the wreck in detail for the first time - but without pain. In my dream I was not an outsider watching the action like in a movie; I was the main character reliving the experience.

I remember laughing. Everything was good. I was driving a big truck with a stick-shift. The floor mats were a dark gray color. Wes King was blaring on the stereo. He was singing "The Robe". I was driving, and I was happy.

All of a sudden the tires began moving strangely; in my head I told myself, "Go to the right! To the right!" because I felt the truck moving to the left. I kept trying hard to turn; I was fighting the steering wheel. I heard a *click*, and the steering wheel began to spin; then another sound - *boom!* - and the truck started flipping. I could feel myself turning and turning with the truck. I felt the glass; I heard it smash. There was no screaming, no voices, just the screech and banging of a wreck in progress. I felt myself move in slow motion as I flew through glass. For a time, I was airborne. I felt an impact, like I'd been hit in my head, then I was rolling; but there was no pain. And suddenly, it was all over.

Above me, below me, all around me was utter darkness. I was lying on solid ground, but it was dark everywhere. Yet there was no fear. I had the strangest, most beautiful feeling ever ... it was like I was where I belonged.

In my dream, I was not lying on my stomach as I had been in the actual wreck. I was on my side, and began to see into the distance on the right. From far away, I could see people - lots of people - people in light. It was indescribably beautiful. I heard laughing, and music - majestic, uplifting music. It was yellow, white, bright, glorious, and sunny. I felt peaceful, and euphoric, that everything was going to be OK.

I tried to get up off the ground to go to that beautiful place of light. I knew in my spirit I belonged with those people. My body was lying there, and I was trying to move, but I couldn't.

Then I saw Him walk over to me. He had on a long tunic and sandals with golden-like straps. His hair was long and bushy. His eyes were beyond description. He squatted down beside me and touched me - and He talked to me. We talked for a long time; but I can't remember all that He said. What I do remember Him saying was this:

Nicole, the wreck was not in My perfect will. You were not supposed to be in that wreck. That was not My will. You are not supposed to be here. But you are here. A lot of people are praying for you. People need you. Your husband needs you. I put you together with Jason because there is no one else who can help him fulfill My perfect will. But right now, you are here. So I'm going to let you decide.

I don't remember saying anything to Him. I could only hear Him. But apparently, I said, or at least I thought and He heard me, "I will go back."

And He said to me: *You have a very long and hard road ahead of you now. But I will be with you every step of the way. I promise.*

I woke from my sleep, still tied up to the bed in the room on the 8th floor, my pillow still wet with the tears that had gone cold. But I felt calmer. The dream gave me peace, and hope. Jesus had shown me what had happened in the wreck, so I wouldn't always wonder. He gave me purpose to move forward, and reminded me that people were praying for me. I no longer felt alone. I no longer feared dying - in fact, I wanted more than ever to be with Jesus.

I remembered His words, thought about them over and over, and clung to them with a blessed assurance. *People need you. Your husband needs you. ... You have a very long and hard road ahead of you now. But I will be with you every step of the way. I promise.*

Jason returned to the hospital that evening to spend the night in my room. When he walked in, he stopped, looked into my eyes, and saw that something had changed. He said, "I'm getting my Nicole back. She's coming back."

CHAPTER EIGHT

Learning to Live Again

Unless the LORD had been my help, My soul would soon have settled in silence. - Psalm 94:17 (NKJV)

If your life is broken, it may be because pieces will feed a multitude. - Elisabeth Elliot

YOU CAN PROBABLY imagine that the cost of being hospitalized in the United States for almost three months was phenomenal. We were faced with bills that came to $290,000 USD, owed to 19 different physicians. Attorneys would come to visit me often, wanting to know if we were going to sue. I guess I could have been a millionaire, but as Christians we were advised not to sue.

It took us 14 years to finally pay off the debt. We'd make small payments so that we could continue what we were doing on the mission field. Jason's mom was the main one who helped us deal with the payments. I will never forget what an enormous help my mother-in-law was to us. She wrote checks every month for many years while we sometimes struggled to pay those bills. But we were also blessed to be helped by donors, and some of the doctors graciously forgave our debt; others made sure we would not go into total financial hardship.

I hardly remember Jason's mom being at the hospital - or my dad either, for that matter, even though both of them stayed for the first two months and faithfully visited me every day. Dad read to me from the Bible. It became impossible for them to stay any longer, but for most of the time they were there I was unconscious, or at best, semi-conscious. Then my mother-in-law went back to Missouri, and my dad, who was still a full-time missionary, returned to Peru to carry on the work there. Mom, my brothers, and my little sister stayed with me.

The vision of my wreck and of Jesus that I had that day in the hospital was ongoing - it didn't just happen once. Every time I woke up, every time I went to sleep, for years, I had the same vision. I would still see Jesus; I would feel His presence, saying *I will be with you every step of the way*. It comforted me beyond description.

As I've mentioned earlier, a verse that has helped me time and again over the years, as I think back on so many experiences, is this: *And we know that God causes all things to work together for good to those who love God, to those who are called according to His purpose*.[7] I can see this throughout the circumstances of the wreck and how God turned so much pain around. This is not to say that everything became rosy and wonderful and I am now pain-free and completely healed. Far from it! But there is so much that God has done in and through my accident that I am astounded at His love and grace.

For example, you might be wondering what happened to our truck. Jason donated the diesel engine from the truck, in

---

7. Romans 8:28, NASB (italics mine)

order for a big airboat to be built for my Daddy to use in bringing the gospel to the unreached people in the Amazon jungles.
That same vehicle I'd wrecked was able to provide for my Dad's
ministry in ways we could not have imagined! I treasure the
pictures I have of the huge airboat, operated by the Cummins
diesel engine, with my parents and other Peruvian missionaries preaching the gospel! It was a wonderful way in which God
took the tragedy and turned it into blessing and kingdom opportunities.

As I continued to recover, the Lord often encouraged me
through the blessing of a visit from family or friends or a Bible verse written inside a handmade card. Yet recovery continued to be a daily struggle. I came to realize that every single as-
pect of my life had changed. Physically, I had terrible problems
from the top of my head down to my knees. Mentally, I was not
the same person I used to be. Emotionally, I had no idea how
to react to new things. And so there were many new fears and
insecurities that I'd never had before, including the fear of going outside.

My physical therapist helped me so much. She was a sweet
tiny lady from the Philippines with a big belly - she was pregnant. I had physical therapy with her every morning and afternoon. After my period of depression this wonderful woman would put me in a wheelchair and push me outside, to the
back of the hospital. I had no memory of trees, or grass, or anything outdoors. The physical therapist gently helped me out of
the wheelchair and sat me down on the grass for a long time,
and I just contemplated the new world all around me - the day-
light instead of the artificial hospital lights, the people coming
in and out of the hospital, the highway, the noises, the sky.

There were moments during the period of rehab when I was
given "recess": I was allowed to leave the hospital and spend a
few hours at the Trujillos' beach house with Jason, away from

the hospital and the constant medical atmosphere. The first time I was given recess and left the hospital was truly harrowing. It was a much bigger shock than I was expecting.

We'd used our wrecked truck's insurance money to purchase another one like it. Jason had driven up to Wisconsin to retrieve it at a cheaper price from a retired missionary co-worker - if you can believe it, it was a 1992 Cummings Diesel, exactly the same model and make as the one I'd crashed, only a different color. Getting up into it was painful - and unsettling. *What if we crashed?* I was overwhelmed by everything around me. As we drove through the center of the town and sat in noisy traffic, we passed people everywhere - some smiling, some irritated; I felt vulnerable, looking at all the shops and people carrying bags of stuff, hearing people shout and car horns blaring and Jason talking to me ... It was a definite case of sensory overload.

As we began to drive over the massive Harbor Bridge towards the beach house, my heart started to flutter. "Jason, please stop the truck," I said. "I'm afraid - I'm scared." Jason couldn't stop - not in the middle of the bridge. I closed my eyes, gripping the armrest with one hand and the dashboard with the other. My breathing became shallow. I felt my heart pounding and my skin go prickly on the back of my neck and arms. That bridge was just too high for me.

I started to breathe again once we were down the other side, driving slowly towards the beach house, which was a simple building in a group of units, with a clear view of blue sky and the beach, across a large green lawn. The simplicity of the area, the fresh breeze, and the little house gave me peace.

During those times of recess out of the hospital with Jason, it was as if we were newlyweds all over again - except it was not the same. I had to learn how to love my husband again; how to kiss him; how to let him hold me; how to be intimate with him. This was terribly difficult for both Jason and me. What can it be but the grace of God that we came through all of these challenges?

I thank God that my husband stood by me through all the suffering, confusion, tension and awkwardness. I know that God gave me that dream so that I could start to move forward; He told me that Jason needed me, that together we would do something great for Him. I believe that this was the root that held our marriage firm, and our hearts steady. Just as Jason had set about to help me remember him and to win my heart again, so God had given me the assurance that we were to serve Him together, and in this way my own heart turned toward loving Jason again.

And this stability as a married couple was needed. People continued to come and say things without thinking about their implications or how we might take them to heart.

"Oh, that was the old Nicole. That's what you used to do. You'll never do that again."

It's interesting how that worked. There came a point when the more people said things like that to me (and they really thought they were right), the more determined I became to prove them wrong. I started trying hard to walk again, with the help of the back brace and walker. They said, "You were so strong and athletic; you could do anything. Oh well ... you'll *never* be able to jump rope again. You used to be able to do 5000 jumps a day."

Well, within a year, I was doing 5000 jumps a day again. Their negative words pushed me to do the impossible.

"You'll probably *never* be able to bench press more than what you weigh." *Sigh.*

Within two years, I was bench pressing a whole lot more than what I weighed. If I had actually believed what these people were saying, I might not have come through the way I did. I had to make a choice between listening to them, or listening to what God had already told me. In the end, those words did not take root. God's words took root and I clung to them for strength.

Nevertheless, there came a point well before this, while I was still in rehab, when the head doctor in charge of the Rehab floor came to see me. It was late March, almost three months after my accident. I was still losing weight, unable to keep food down. I looked terrible. In reality, I was getting worse, not better. (It was discovered later that my gallbladder had shut down from having a feeding tube for so long, but this was not attended to at the right time.) The doctor looked at me for a long time with a concerned expression and asked me, "What do you want, Nicole? What will make you happy?"

"I want to go home," I told him in a small voice.

"Where *is* your home?" he asked. I couldn't answer - I didn't know where my home was. I think God must have prompted me to say it. The doctor looked at me kindly. "I am going to send you home, Nicole," he said. "We really can't do anything else for you here. You can go home. I hope that'll help you. Y'all come back in one month and we'll see how you're doing and take it from there."

* * *

The doctor allowed me to leave the hospital with Jason. We drove all the way down to the Freedom Ministries base in Raymondville, Texas. We stayed there for a month while I was given regular outpatient rehab therapy at Valley Baptist Medical Center in Harlingen, half an hour away.

There were a lot of missionary families staying at Raymondville, having been evacuated from Mexico due to the uprising in Chiapas. They were deeply focused on the problems Mexico was facing, and trying to make decisions for the future.

I think hardly anyone realized how bad off I was. I was still barely walking at all, and heavily dependent on others for help with almost everything. During these weeks, I was often left alone. Not even Jason could be with me all the time, as the mission began sending him back to Mexico to care for our house churches we had pioneered. The weather was starting to warm up, which fatigued me even more, and I was on my own more times than I really should have been.

When Jason wasn't with me, I would stay at Debbie Hogan's house, and when no-one else could, she'd drive me to Harlington for the therapies.

There was one occasion when Mrs Debbie picked me up after therapy. She was busy, as always, but she stopped by a Subway fast food shop to grab a bite to eat. "I have *got* to get myself a Cold Cut Combo," she said to me. "Can I get you anything, honey?" I asked for one of the same, with all the salads and garnish. Debbie took the two combos and handed one to me.

I took one bite. "What do you think?" Debbie asked me.

I smiled, with a mouthful of food. "I love it!" I replied. To her surprise - and mine - I ate the entire 6 inch sub! It was the first item of food I'd eaten in months - and actually kept down! Debbie was amazed.

Back at Debbie's place later that afternoon, as I slowly made my way into her kitchen after a long nap, I discovered an array of food - every single ingredient from the Cold Cut Combo - carefully prepared and laid out on her kitchen counter. I was amazed. "Mrs. Debbie! What's all this food for?" I called out to her.

Debbie came in, smiling widely. "Honey, you ate real food for the first time in months. So if you want to make another one, don't ask permission. You make one whenever you want. We need to get you eating and feeling better. That's all that matters."

There were few people who fully supported me and encouraged me during this time of outpatient rehab. My fellow missionary friends Judy, Lisa, Leigh Ann, Ellie, Brenda, Lisa, Cindi and Crystal were all supportive though, in many ways. But the Hogans helped me whenever I needed it. They were the ones who would say to me, "Don't you care one bit about other people's opinions about yourself. The only opinion you need to care about is Jesus', and He just loves you so much."

On April 29th, I returned to Corpus Christi with Jason for my final revision, with all my main doctors coming to see me. They were all delighted to see that I was doing better. Dr. Zanetti, the neurologist, assessed me again with a series of questions and physical tests to make sure he could sign with confidence that I was mentally and physically ready to leave and able to begin to live fully in the real world once again.

"Nicole, I'm going to ask you the same questions I asked you before. Are you ready? Who was President of the United States when you were born?"

"Gerald Ford," I replied. It was crazy. *How did I know that?* I thought to myself. I didn't even know my own birthday!

The doctor ticked something on the paper attached to his clipboard and continued. "Very good. Which famous President died recently?"

"Richard Nixon", I said. Jason looked at me, his eyebrows raised in surprise, but with a smile forming on his face. I still felt amazed. I didn't consciously know the answer to this question. Yet, somehow, I gave the doctor the right answer to *every single question* he asked! Then came the physical exam. I had to stand on my tiptoes, then lean on my heels and keep my balance. I did everything he asked me to do. I'm sure it was the Holy Spirit, helping me at every point of the exam. I was still wearing my back brace, but I was deemed "competent".

The doctor signed my release form, and then he did something he rarely did to any of his patients. He gave me a hug.

"You *almost* make me believe there is a God," he said to me, holding my shoulders and smiling at me.

"Doctor Zanetti, there *is* a God!" I replied confidently, smiling back. "I am living, walking proof that God exists and that He is able to do more than we could ever ask or imagine!"

* * *

We stayed in Raymondville for two more weeks after my release from the hospital, and began to prepare for our return to Mexico in May. Who would have imagined that within less than 5 months after that horrific accident and all that followed, we'd be heading back to do mission work again?

Was it too early for us to do this? Looking back, I'd say yes, it almost certainly was. Yet my family and our mission group were all go-getters; they just weren't the type to tell anyone to take anything slowly. My mom, who'd been my rock during the entire hospital experience, had to get back to Peru to be with Dad. Jason was being called to go back full-time into evangelism and church planting. And there was another factor: some missionaries had permanently left Mexico because of the conflict and decided to remain in the US. So there was a lot of pressure to keep hold of those missionaries who were willing to return, and to send them back to Mexico as soon as possible.

More terrible events had happened in Mexico since the Zapatista uprising in the south. On March 23, 1994, the presidential candidate for the ruling party and the favorite to win, Luis Donaldo Colosio, was brutally assassinated at a campaign rally in Tijuana. This threw the country into even more unrest.

As a result of all this, and for security reasons, we were assigned by our mission to work and live with other missionaries. The ministry put three or four families together in one house or on one block, and we had a curfew. Although this sometimes complicated things, on the whole life was good during that time.

We lived with Cindi and Crystal in Huejutla de Reyes. Cindi Hogan was our good friend, married to Jo-D at our double wedding of 18 months before. Crystal was Jo-D's younger sister, finishing high school. Both of these wonderful young women helped me through all the areas of life as a woman and a wife in Mexico: how to peel a carrot, cook a meal, clean the house, go grocery shopping, buy medicine, wash clothes - everything.

There was still so much to learn, but amongst all the hard work we had a lot of fun. We played a lot of board games. I used to be a whiz at games like Axis & Allies and Trivial Pursuit; now, anything that required strategic thinking or general knowledge of the world was totally out of the question for me. Instead, we played games that didn't need a lot of knowledge or skill: Monopoly, Battleship, and Pictionary (they gave me extra time to look up the words in a dictionary and think about how I could draw them).

On one occasion, I was fixing myself a treat I'd seen someone else make: I put peanut butter onto a peeled banana. I couldn't remember eating this before, but it looked tasty. I was about to take the first bite when Cindi walked in and shouted, "DON'T EAT THAT!"

"Why? What's wrong?" I asked, alarmed, the banana in my hand.

"You *hate* peanut butter! It makes you sick - you'll throw that up the minute you swallow it!"

I stopped and thought about it. Cindi was one of my closest friends and I knew she wouldn't lie to me. But I had no recollection of violently hating peanut butter. I took a bite - and liked it. I ate the whole banana.

Six months after having left the hospital, I had more surgery on the vertebrae in my back. The neurologist and orthopedic surgeons wanted me walking brace-free within a year. The surgery was supposed to be only 45 minutes long, but it turned into 6 full hours, as my bone had grown very quickly and had covered the rods that were bracing my vertebrae. The surgeons had to do a lot of work to release the rods. Since it was so unusual, they asked my permission to share my story and pictures in a medical book.

In the fall of that first year we traveled to Louisiana, to visit family. We went to my Aunt Michelle's house. Aunt Michelle had been with my parents in the hospital on that fateful New Year's Eve. She was like a big sister to me, a mentor, and a constant role model for me. She greeted me with great enthusiasm and hugs at her front door. I held onto her hand as I walked slowly inside; as we entered her living room I heard a great shout of "SURPRISE!"

There in front of me were my Grandma, some aunts and uncles, cousins, friends, even a couple of friends from churches I'd been to. The room was filled with people, all so excited to see me. The problem was that I didn't know them. They'd made all my favorite food dishes, apparently, although I didn't know it. And the noise, the number of people all coming up to me, talking to me, trying to make me remember - it was overwhelming, another case of sensory overload.

My head stopped registering the words as people talked to me - they were just buzzing sounds. I found it hard to breathe. I had to get outside, away from everyone; in a daze I pushed open the front door and stood on the grass with my eyes closed, trying to breathe, waiting for my panic attack to go down. I didn't want to hurt anyone's feelings, but it was impossible to go back inside. After a little while I could hear car doors closing as people began to leave. Aunt Michelle came out to stand next to me and put her arm around me. She was very sorry, and very sad that she'd unthinkingly created something so hard for me to cope with.

I was recovering, that was certain; but I couldn't go at anyone else's pace but my own.

CHAPTER NINE

Dusty Boxes and Dirt Trails

...Not lagging behind in diligence, fervent in spirit, serving the Lord; rejoicing in hope, persevering in tribulation, devoted to prayer, contributing to the needs of the saints, practicing hospitality. - Romans 12:11-13 (NASB)

People do not care how much you know until they know how much you care. [Heard spoken at a U.S. Marine base I visited during one of the many graduation ceremonies for my son]

WE RETURNED TO Mexico on May 14th, 1994. Two months later, in July, our mission organization finally regarded it safe for missionaries to live on their own again; so we moved to the house that we'd been planning to settle into, in Xochiatipan, over seven months before. There were more big shocks in store for me here when we arrived: boxes and boxes of stuff that we'd hurriedly dumped there back in December 1993 before our "quick trip" to Texas and Chiapas. Now they awaited my opening each one and discovering more about who Nicole Fitzpatrick used to be - or perhaps still was, who could tell?

The house itself was unfinished, with a concrete floor but missing doors and windows. We were totally in the boondocks! There was no electricity, no running water, no fridge, gas stove, or lights - we had to use candles at night. I had to learn to be resourceful with food so that it wouldn't go bad. We filled up buckets of water for washing dishes and for flushing the toilet.

To wash clothes, I'd walk down the hill from our house to the public washing area known as the *lavaderos*. This was a large circular well filled with water and a series of cement ridges nearby, where the women would scrub their clothes and rinse them off by dipping a container into the clean well water and pouring it over the soapy clothes. Then I'd have to carry the wet clothes back up the steep hill to hang up at my house.

When the weather was wet, it would take me 1-2 hours to walk carefully down the slippery hill, wash the clothes and carry the wet items back to our house - even longer when I washed the heavy blankets. I had to walk slowly, one cautious step at a time, so as not to skid and hurt myself.

Our situation without electricity lasted for a year, and we had no running water or windows for almost two years. It was like going back into missionary life of the past, 100 years earlier. I actually liked it; I was able to set up my house, little by little, buying pieces of furniture, including my first rocking chair which I loved dearly.

However, living on our own was an enormous challenge for me mentally as well as physically - I found myself once again left to work things out in an adult world, but with the mind of a young girl, and with no-one around us. I set about continuing to recover, learn, and create a steady routine, reminding myself that routine brought stability. At the beginning it was still difficult and painful to walk, so I mostly stayed home, reading the Bible and writing. I submerged myself in the Word of God, reading entire books or two epistles in one day. I loved this time - there was a lot of peace and quiet and I could sit and look out the window at the beautiful green mountains as I prayed, studied the Bible, and worked on my calligraphy.

Back in the 80s I had very pretty handwriting; after the wreck, I had no hand-eye coordination and could hardly write at all. In the 90s, with no cell phones or computers, all our letters and communications were handwritten, so I would do exercises in tracing letters in order to improve my writing and be able to write letters to our family and partners. Calligraphy was the only thing I wanted to do well.

Apparently, before my accident I loved to cross-stitch and knit; people would bring me items I'd made for them in the past to try to convince me that I was really good at it. But I'd lost my love for all those things.

At one point a dear friend brought me a 500-piece jigsaw puzzle of a parrot, because I used to love puzzles. But even though I wanted to, my mind was simply unable to do it. I would sit for hours staring at one puzzle piece and wondering where it might go. The puzzle might as well have had 5000 pieces! There was no way I could do it, and it caused pressure on my brain, giving me headaches. Finally Jason, seeing my frustration, put it together for me in less than an hour. We still have that finished parrot puzzle.

During those days, I would look at the large pile of dusty bags and boxes that belonged to us and open them slowly, not with excitement, but with a reluctant indifference. I read through the journal I used to write in - but only with a mild interest, as if I'd been told I had to read somebody else's journal. But it was a little bit irritating, too, because it sounded like it *could* have been me, and yet I didn't feel like it *was* me.

At one point I opened a box full of dried petals and leaves. I sighed and rolled my eyes. "Why on earth do I have this?" I wondered to myself. I put it into the pile of things to burn - the things I didn't want to keep or couldn't see a need for anymore.

A few years later, Jason and I were talking, and he commented on a big box of potpourri I used to have.

"Potpourri? What's that?" I asked, puzzled.

"Well, it's like dried flowers with fragrance oils on them. And what you did was, you made a big box of potpourri out of every flower I'd ever given you since we met. And you kept that box in our room. And you said for your whole life you were gonna -" he stopped talking and frowned in thought. "Where is that box?"

I had to tell him. "I burned it. I thought it was a box of old, ratty petals."

I couldn't see it at the time - they held no value for me at all, and I didn't see the point of a missionary keeping a box like that. But now, when I think about it, I get sentimental. Four years worth of roses and pretty flowers - everything he'd ever bought me - burned up as if it were nothing.

In another box labeled *Hospital Stuff,* I discovered a very beautiful, elegant bracelet. It was full of pretty jewels of many different colors. I didn't know where the bracelet had come from or what it had to do with my being in the hospital. When a little girl we knew from the village was having a birthday, I wrapped it up and gave it to her. Yes, this was yet another time when I misjudged the value of something.

A long time later, Jason and my Mom were talking about things that had happened over the years, and they mentioned the bracelet that I'd had on my wrist at the hospital. Not having any memory of it, I said, "Huh?" Then I did remember that I'd given away a beautiful bracelet to a poor little girl, years earlier. Jason and Mom were shocked.

"That bracelet was the real deal, Nicole! Those weren't *pretend* jewels! They were real rubies, real sapphires, emeralds, diamonds, you name it!" exclaimed Jason, astounded.

It turned out that Saul, the former drug dealer at Memorial Medical Center in Corpus Christi, had brought it to me and gifted it to me. Personally I had never met Saul, being in a coma while he'd been at the hospital, but he'd written me a letter "for when I got better", and Jason had told me about him later. We'll probably never know what happened to Saul after he left the hospital. But we sure hope and pray he stayed faithful to God till the end - and that the bracelet might have brought great blessing to that little girl.

About ten years ago I watched a movie called *The Vow*, based on a true story about a young newlywed couple involved in a car accident in which the wife goes to the hospital in a coma and wakes up with amnesia. As I watched it, at almost every scene I marveled and thought, "I can't believe it! This movie is the story of my life!" The fact that she couldn't remember she was married, that her husband had to win back her love, that she ate food she used to dislike, that there was hurt and confusion and moments where everything was overwhelming ... I often felt so alone, so different, yet the wife in the movie had the same experiences I did. It helped me realize my experience was common to other people as well.

There were crazy moments, especially when we'd travel to the villages in the mountains to preach the gospel. We hiked a lot - straight up mountains. I was slowly getting stronger and fitter, but those hikes along narrow dirt trails were hard. Jason often walked behind me, holding my back as we walked up. When he couldn't do that, he'd walk ahead of me, and I'd hold onto his belt loops. Gently pushing or pulling me, we'd make it up the mountains to get to those remote places. Other times we'd go on Jason's motorcycle and we'd ride together. When it was possible, we'd drive a truck. We spent a lot of time washing the big trucks and tightening bolts that had come loose from the rough roads.

On the whole, while physically it was a challenging life, it wasn't stressful. People smiled at each other on the street and brought meals around if a neighbor was sick or grieving; they rejoiced and congratulated the family who'd just had a baby. People cared for each other. They observed us and what we would do to help the poorest of the village. I ministered to a lot of unwed mothers, giving them food and bags of clothes we brought down from the USA. I kept some large Rubbermaid containers in our living room which I'd fill with rice, beans, lentils, and sugar, and every week I'd give care packages to the widows and the unwed mothers of the village.

Xochiatipan was a primitive place in many aspects - the Nahuatl people mixed together old superstitions and witchcraft beliefs and practices with the old Roman Catholic traditions of veneration of saints and idols. In Jason's preaching and my sharing we fought against the two main problems of false religion and alcoholism; this second one was destroying many families in the village, but both led to bondage and hopelessness.

The care of the Xochiatipan people was very visible especially when people from other villages would oppose what Jason was doing in preaching the gospel or showing the Jesus film in public. At times violent men grabbed him - or even worse, tried to shoot him, or picked up rocks and stoned him - in order to make him stop. But the people of our village, even though they held fast to the beliefs of their fathers, would always stand with us to protect us.

"Look, I'm not saying we accept their religion, but they're not harming us," they'd say, speaking up for us. "They're helping the poor. They love people. They're doing a good thing."

Why was there opposition? It was because Jason was bringing something totally new in preaching Jesus. This might sound weird, considering that Mexico is a predominantly Catholic country, at least in theory. But the gospel was being presented in a way they'd never heard before. The only Jesus the people in the villages had ever known of was either the baby Jesus, helpless and indefensive in His mother Mary's arms; or else the weak, dying Jesus hanging on a cross, with His loving mother Mary at its foot.

Either way, the emphasis was more on Mary than on Jesus, and many times God was thought of as an angry, unapproachable father. For hundreds of years, the people have had a religion that looks to Mary (or the Virgin of Guadalupe, who is a mixed version of a Nahuatl mother goddess and "brown-skinned" virgin Mary - as many Mexicans call her) to go to God on behalf of her children. In this religion, Jesus really has no importance or relevance at all.

So, when Jason began to preach Jesus, at first the people would be interested, because they'd heard about someone called Jesus before. But they didn't like changing their traditions, and so although they weren't always hostile and angry, they would frequently chase away the preacher, and sometimes try to kill him. Jason was often stoned by villagers as he drove away on his motorcycle after preaching in a church. I'd come out to meet him when I heard his motorcycle come up to our house, and he'd get off his bike with cuts or bruises, his helmet dented from the rocks. This didn't happen just once or twice - it was a common thing.

There were some terribly tough places where Jason took the gospel. People in some towns produced their own distinct type of strong alcohol known as *aguardiente* (firewater). It was a type of moonshine, and it's what all the people in that village would drink. In most places the culture was just to keep drinking until you dropped - the concept of drinking in moderation was not heard of. They always drank too much. How the people loved their aguardiente! And how the producers loved the money they made from selling it! Yet God saved a lot of those producers and consumers of aguardiente through Jason's preaching ... and miracles happened.

In one place, one of the producers had a wife who was having a difficult pregnancy, in labor for two days. She was hemorrhaging, and there came a point when people thought she had died. But Jason prayed for her and she was healed; the baby was born, and the husband gave his life to Christ! Like Saul the ex-drug dealer, he was convicted by the Holy Spirit and he stopped producing the aguardiente. That upset the whole village. Where were they going to get their alcohol from now? They threatened Jason and told him to leave their village.

There were many other times when people of the village would become Christians, and stop their drinking. The revenue would decrease; so the producers of aguardiente would start rumors and lies about Christians, and begin to persecute them. It would remind me of the story in Acts of a slave girl who was freed from being possessed by fortune-telling demons, and her owners realized that their source of income had dried up, so they made up rumors about Paul and Silas and incited the authorities to arrest them.[8]

And again, in other cases there was witchcraft involved. A man or a woman would be born again, and the town would begin to panic when they saw how their lives had changed. In one incident there was a man who had gotten drunk, hit his head, and become paralyzed for the entire day. Some people took Jason to see him. The man was conscious and could talk, but he was unable to move. Jason preached the gospel to him, he believed and was saved, and got up! He was able to run, and his strength quickly returned.

---

8. Acts 16:16-24

The problem was, his mother was a witch.

She began going door to door and telling people, "I was doing my magic and he was healed. That man's god didn't heal him - I healed him!" She made a lot of noise, and commanded the attention of the people. They wanted to kill Jason. "He's a white man! A foreigner! He's here for your women, and for your children!" the woman would shout. "He's talking about a different god! He's from the devil! That's not Jesus he's preaching - it's a different Jesus." It didn't make a lot of sense, but the people believed her.

Jason left on his motorbike, bombarded by large rocks thrown by the children and the men of the town. *Bang, bang, bang*, went the rocks on his helmet.

But it was also common that people became more open to listening to the gospel message through someone from the village opening up their house to having meetings, and someone being healed. A good part of the house churches Jason started came as a result of healings. He would hear of a child or a parent who was sick, paralyzed, feverish, or dying of cancer, and he'd go into the house and lay hands on them, pleading the blood of Jesus to heal them - and they would be healed by the power of God. When this happened, the people would stop and listen, and their harsh treatment would cease. By God's grace and mercy, Jason established many house churches, and many people gave their lives to Jesus.

* * *

At first, my whole life revolved around Jason: cooking, cleaning, making his favorite dessert, keeping the house looking beautiful for him to come back to. I was the secretary, sending thank-you letters to our supporters. As my handwriting improved, I was able to write 30 or 40 letters by hand every month to our supporters. I also prayed a lot. Having witnessed so many times the power of prayer, I spent hours on my knees, interceding for others. Jason and I prayed together every morning; I would pray for one or two hours every evening while Jason was gone. We lifted up prayer for our family, the planted churches, the people we were ministering to, and for Mexico.

We also prayed for children. And God heard and answered our prayer.

Chapter Ten

Family

And they said to Him, "Do You hear what these children are saying?" And Jesus said to them, "Yes. Have you never read, 'From the mouths of infants and nursing babies You have prepared praise for Yourself'?" - Matthew 21:16 (NASB)

The child is the beauty of God present in the world, that greatest gift to a family. - Mother Teresa

FROM THE DAY we were married, Jason and I had been greatly looking forward to starting a family. It was a terrible blow for us when, after the wreck, the hospital doctors told me that my reproductive system had gone into shock from the injuries, and that I would probably never be able to bear children. Even if I did get pregnant, they advised me to have an abortion, because my weak back could never carry a pregnancy to term.

We felt devastated by this. I loved children so much. I'd been looking forward to pregnancy, to giving birth to my own children, to holding my newborn baby in my arms and being Mom to my children.

But God. He was not restrained by the dire predictions of doctors. Although my body's rhythms had not settled into a normal routine and I was actually on birth control, I conceived - just 13 months after the wreck! It was not until the third month that I even knew I was pregnant! What amazing news it was. It was such a blessing from the Lord.

It was a simple, easy pregnancy; but due to the number of risk factors, I had an emergency C-section on November 15, 1995, and our beautiful son Sed Justus was born. I looked at Sed in the incubator crib next to my bed, and asked the doctor if he would let me hold him, which he did. The moment I picked up little Sed in my arms and looked into the face of my beautiful firstborn child, my entire life was transformed. I never knew a love that strong could exist. It was almost an ache.

The next evening we got ready to leave the clinic with our baby. As we stood at the counter in order to pay the hospital bill, a young boy, about 12 years old, came into the clinic from off the street. He was so small and lanky, with ragged clothes and thin dirty arms; the skin on his face was dry and cracked, ravaged by the weather. In a voice devoid of any expression or hope, he said to me, "*Una moneda para comprarme un pan*" ("Give me a coin to buy a piece of bread"). I was holding my own precious baby boy in my arms. I looked at this little boy and wondered, *Where is his mother?*

I asked him, "Have you eaten anything today?" He looked at me fully for the first time and shook his head. I gave him more money than he was expecting - enough to eat for a few days. At that moment I didn't question if he might buy something else, like drugs or alcohol - my motherly instinct just surfaced and I ran with it. But I wanted to give him everything; I wanted to give him a home and safety. With a terrible sinking feeling in my heart, I had to walk away.

Little Sed brought us joy, hope, and life. Being a mother

made me feel whole and needed. It filled a void in my life. I loved every moment with Sed, listening to him giggle, playing with him, cuddling him after his nap, reading him stories, singing to him at bedtime. Even so, many times as I nursed Sed, my mind would wander to that little boy who came in off the streets, and I'd wonder where he was and what had happened to him.

* * *

Those were happy years. Jason continued to work preaching the gospel and pioneering new house churches in unreached indigenous villages in central Mexico, and God blessed his ministry. As little groups of new believers grew, I would go along to help him serve these people, especially the women and the children. I'd minister to the Christian ladies and help them cook and answer questions they had about God and Jesus.

We'd sit around a warm wood-fired stove in their little kitchen, grinding fresh corn or using our hands to pat it into tortillas and heating them on the stove, while talking about the Word of God and watching little Sed play with a toy car or with the other kids. It was a great privilege when, in 1998, we were officially honored and made members of the Nahuatl people of nearby Zacatlán Xochiatipan, where years earlier David Hogan had planted a church and where we began the task of building up the believers in discipleship.

When Sed was 3 years old, I miscarried a baby. This was my second miscarriage. Then, a year later, I miscarried again. It was a terribly difficult and uncertain time for Jason and me. We were so unsure whether to keep trying to have another child or not. We prayed a lot for God's guidance, and decided to begin the process of adopting two children instead - a 2-year-old girl from Haiti, and a baby girl from Mexico.

Unbelievably, as we were approaching the final stages

of adoption, I conceived again! We were ecstatic! This didn't change our desire to adopt the two little girls, but the adoption agency halted the process when we told them I was pregnant. We were thankful to hear that both girls were placed into good homes.

This was not such an easy pregnancy. At 3 months, I developed blood clots in my groin and right leg. There was a strong risk that part of a clot might travel up to my lung, heart, or brain and cause an embolism or cardiac arrest. Once again I found myself in Intensive Care - this time in a hospital in Kansas City - and once again I was not expected to live. The doctors advised me it would be better to abort, declaring that neither of us would make it through the pregnancy. I refused to do this; so they monitored the pregnancy through my regular visits to the hospitals in Mexico once we returned, and I controlled the blood clotting by injecting myself with heparin every 12 hours. And we prayed constantly.

Finally, to our great joy, our tiny 5lb (2.26kg) angel Jasmine Elane was born on May 3, 2001. She truly was, and still is, a gift from God. I am very blessed to have these three amazing people as my family - Jason, Sed, and Jasmine.

On most days, Jason would travel to two or three different villages and hold church services or meetings. At the beginning, when our children were small, we would all go with him. But once Sed and Jasmine were of schooling age, I stayed back with them and homeschooled them more often.

There were so many moments when we saw God answering prayer. Some, like Jasmine's birth, were big moments; some were small, but that didn't take away their significance. When Jasmine was little, she asked me for a pair of "purple pajamas with pink monkeys on them. And ruffles." I couldn't forget the ruffles. I'd never heard of such a thing. Purple pajamas with pink monkeys and ruffles? OK. I began searching - everywhere.

I looked in every store I went to in Mexico and the USA. I even searched in fabric stores for the material so I could make the pajamas myself. It was *impossible*. Yet Jasmine wanted them so much. She asked God for those specific pajamas in her prayers every single day, for months.

Then, after Hurricane Katrina struck in 2005, something happened. We volunteered several weeks with Freedom Ministries to help the thousands of hurricane victims in the region of Mississippi and New Orleans. We were working to create relief pods, packing emergency supplies for those who needed it. We had to go through thousands of items of clothes daily - semi trailer loads full of clothes.

One day the police came. Apparently there were trucks coming full of clothes that were going to be dumped, as they'd been sitting for a week and there was risk of contamination. They told us we could keep anything we wanted. *Really?!* We had just a few minutes to look through half a parking lot covered in mountains of clothes. But can you believe what my sweet daughter and I found in the middle of that mountain? The most precious pair of purple pajamas with pink monkeys - and ruffles! Jasmine was ecstatic. I was over the moon. And we held hands, bowed our heads and thanked our Father God for answering her prayer.

* * *

For the majority of the first 10 years or so of our marriage, my life and ministry was dedicated mainly to my family: looking after my husband and children first, ministering to others second. I did whatever I could to keep us united and secure; reading the children stories each night, cuddling them on my rocking chair, gently rubbing their little backs just as my Mama had done for me, taking them on field trips, and including them whenever we all went to minister in a particular area, in the same way that my parents had included us as kids on the mission field. Jasmine and I would often wear a dress or outfit made from the same fabric and color. Together we'd sing kids' songs and have a little church service with the children of the village, using Bible stories and craft activities. Over the years in Xochiatipan, I created a strong children's ministry. And I began taking care of unwed mothers.

To help their families financially, many young people from the villages would go to Mexico City and work there for a while. Often the young girls returned with one or two children, but with no husband. Jason and I would find out later that the girls had gotten pregnant - for some, this would have been without their consent. Most of them had never received any type of sexual education or been prepared for living in a big city and having relationships.

In the end, these young girls would be abandoned by their boyfriends and they'd return to the village, pregnant or with their small children. Many of them were shunned and treated like whores when they returned to the village. People would point their fingers at them and talk about them. Often the grandparents would keep the children and raise them. There would still be no explanation or education, only rejection and disdain.

My heart went out to these women and their children. I hated seeing them suffer. I went to our ministry leaders to ask permission to step up and do something for them. At first, our leadership was not too sure about my intentions. Their mission and ours was not to change their culture or adapt to their culture. We were Americans; they were Mexicans. It was all about preaching Jesus. To a degree, I understood the thoughts of our leaders in the ministry.

But the women and children loved me. I could get closer to them by cooking with them, laughing with them, and playing with the children. The more I did those things, the more connected we became, and I was able to minister to them. I didn't have to change my faith or my culture to get close to them; I was representing Christ to them and they were listening.

I am grateful that our leaders heard me out and allowed me to begin caring for the young unwed mothers and their children. I began feeding them, collecting used clothing for their children, and helping them find more productive jobs. I started having women's Bible studies, prayer meetings, and sessions to help them learn trades. I taught many to bake and decorate cakes to sell, as there was no bakery in Xochiatipan at the time. We had a lot of fun in the kitchen. It was not difficult for me to collect clothes and teach the young women how to bake. God put it in my heart to help them discover who they were as God's beloved daughters, and in Christ learn to forgive themselves and value themselves.

It was a tranquil life, on the whole, for us. I loved that sweet village in the mountains and its simple daily activity. I loved my house, and my flower pots filled with beautiful flowers: jasmines, gardenias, lilies, roses, camellias, poppies, tulips, and many other beauties that I'd lovingly cared for. I was still struggling to overcome my amnesia, but kept working hard to remember and to exercise my brain. I also exercised my body, working out a lot to get strong and fit, and I continued with spiritual disciplines of fasting and praying.

However, it took time for me to realize that my accident had made me a lot more timid and fearful than I was before. I smiled, but I rarely laughed out loud. I didn't like change - I craved stability and routine. For 11 years I was content simply to be a housewife, mother, and missionary helper. I didn't feel the desire, or the need, to speak out loudly or protest against injustice or sin. My voice was small, almost non-existent, and I felt pretty happy to stay in this situation.

But God was about to move me out of this, and give me a voice and a calling that would be used to pull people out of Hell itself.

CHAPTER ELEVEN

The Move

And Jesus came up and spoke to them, saying, "All authority in heaven and on earth has been given to Me. Go, therefore, and make disciples of all the nations, baptizing them in the name of the Father and the Son and the Holy Spirit, teaching them to follow all that I commanded you; and behold, I am with you always, to the end of the age." - Matthew 28:18-20 (NASB)

God will ensure my success in accordance with His plan, not mine. - Francis Chan

IN 2003, SHORTLY before Jasmine's 2nd birthday, our leader David Hogan announced to the missionaries that he felt God wanted them to "expand the mission's territory". Three men were chosen to pioneer new areas in Mexico; Jason was one of them. Having successfully planted many house churches in the region surrounding Xochiatipan - all of which were now being overseen by national pastors - Jason was asked to move out again into pioneer work. It was a great blessing to know that other national missionaries could visit those house churches from time to time, and that the churches were now established and mature enough to sustain themselves and continue to grow.

However, for me personally it was a blow. Almost all my married life had been in Xochiatipan, my children had been born there, the church that we'd planted with God's help had just started construction, and my women's ministry was strong and healthy.

The entire mission fasted for 21 days as we sought the Lord for guidance in our decision making. Jason felt God calling him south, into the state of Puebla. We checked it out on some huge maps that Jason had purchased, spreading them out on our table and peering at the small towns and villages down dirt roads and up mountains.

We packed some bags and began scouting the region. We'd head to a hotel of sorts in the area, and Jason would travel around, stopping in each village and trying to find out if there were any Christians there, if it had already been evangelized, or if there was no gospel input there at all. Then he'd put stars on the map according to the needs of the areas. These villages were mostly made up of people who spoke Nahuatl or Totonaco.

Jason decided on a place called Ahuacatlán, and made plans to move us all there. But when the mission next met together, it turned out that a fellow missionary and dear friend, Britt Hancock, had decided on a nearby town called Cuetzalan. Freedom Ministries had a policy about missionaries not being situated too close together. Jason had to choose a different place, and eventually decided on Tenango de las Flores. This made us feel uncertain; was this really from the Lord? We had to trust.

The day came when Jason made the announcement: "We're leaving in June."

I knew we'd all prayed. I knew Jason was convinced it was the right thing to do. I knew that I was called to serve the Lord and not my own interests or desires. But it didn't stop my stomach from knotting up and the dread I felt about leaving my beloved village. I cried often as we began to pack up our clothes and all our belongings. I tried to cry privately so as not to make Sed or Jasmine upset or confused.

On the day we left Xochiatipan, we packed all we owned into a Ford F450. Everything fit - all except for my beautiful plants. There were about 30 plants that I'd been taking care of for years. I was at a loss as to how to take them with me - I really wanted to. But they didn't fit. Jason said, "We'll have to leave them here, Nicole. Get rid of them. Give them away."

We had neighbors all around us. I began to pass them out to them, smiling at each of these dear people and giving them a hug and a blessing, even as tears rolled down my cheeks. I gave them the beautiful flowering plants and all the herbs. I hoped that in some way the plants would remind them of me.

It was a warm, sunny morning when we left Xochiatipan - but I was crying. I didn't weep or bawl; I just held my kids tight, looking forward, the tears silently flowing down. Everything was blurry. I kept telling myself, *Don't look back. Don't be like Lot's wife. Don't look back!* It seemed so important at the time. I almost felt like I really would turn into a pillar of salt if I did.

I didn't look back. I went forward - to one more town. And as we left, I heard the Lord whisper to me gently, that my favorite flower would be waiting for me.

Growing up in Louisiana, in southern USA, I was surrounded by magnolias: stunning big trees with large, shiny dark-green leaves and large white flowers whose light, sweet fragrance relaxes the senses. I love them so much! It was just one other thing I had to give up upon becoming a missionary, although my heart always rejoiced when I could see them again on visits back to the South. I missed them in Mexico. I found it a little hard to believe that God was telling me that my favorite flower would be there, in Mexico, waiting for me.

Very late that same night, we arrived in the town called Tenango de las Flores. This is in the northernmost part of Puebla state, with beautiful forests and mountains. The small town is located in between two massive lakes, and is a hub for its production of ornamental flowers. At that time, there were also a lot of towns and villages in the region that had never heard the gospel.

The morning after we arrived, a sweet little neighbor knocked on our door. She had a very old, thin dress on, and was walking awkwardly in broken sandals. She'd brought a gift for us. It was a small magnolia tree for me to plant. My heart swelled. I received it with a big smile and tears in my eyes. I felt so blessed that my Heavenly Father had shown His love for me through this lovely neighborly woman.

* * *

As we began settling in, Jason immediately began going out on his motorcycle to the neighboring villages. He went up against much opposition. He got arrested and shot at many times in those early years. People would cut down trees to block the road into their village in order to stop those who came to share the gospel. It was a dangerous time for him, but he remained faithful and bravely continued to go out.

About six months later, we rejoiced with our first baptisms in a small town called Caxapotla, not far from Tenango. We had a small service, and Jason shared the meaning of baptism for the family members who accompanied the five men and one woman who were immersed in the water.

Baptism is a massive step of faith for indigenous people, especially if they're the first ones to break from their syncretistic pagan-Catholic traditions; they suffer harsh consequences for making that public declaration of becoming a "Protestant". In a sense, baptism in these parts of Mexico is like painting a target on your chest. But what an amazing blessing, to see people declaring their salvation through faith in Jesus Christ!

During that day, as we ate little snacks prepared by some of the sisters of those baptized, I remember feeling a breakthrough - a freedom and awakening. It was as if a darkness that had covered this area for centuries was starting to be pushed back.

We will never forget one incident of gospel resistance. It was about two years after moving to Tenango de las Flores. I was at home with Jasmine. Jason, Sed (who was about 10) and some of the national missionaries went in our truck to Zempoala, a small indigenous village nestled high in the lush mountains of Puebla. It was a place where basically everyone from 40 years and over was illiterate, gripped by their local religion of idols and spiritism.

The entire village of Zempoala - dozens and dozens of people - came out angrily to confront the small group on their arrival; witchdoctors, women who taught catechism, housewives, men with ropes, machetes, sticks, and big rocks. They surrounded the truck. The missionaries remained in the vehicle as angry parishioners threatened to kill them all.

They yelled at Jason in no uncertain terms, "We don't want your gospel! No! We've warned you before. We've cut trees down to block your way. We've told you to stop. You're dead! We're going to kill you."

Jason rolled the window down and tried to converse with them while Sed and the other missionaries stayed quiet, praying under their breath. Jason asked the people why they were upset, and then spoke to them about the Word of God. The people responded with more anger. Jason shared a Bible verse. Some people had their guns cocked and others were getting the ropes ready. Jason didn't fight with them. He just made it abundantly clear: "You people do what you want to do and I'll do what I've come to do."

But two things happened which swung the situation around. An older man called Joaquin and his family inexplicably came closer and asked Jason to tell them more about Jesus. Then a young man walked to the front of the group and pulled a little booklet out of his pocket. It was the Political Constitution of the United States of Mexico.[5]

As the people were still holding their stones, machetes and ropes, the young man began to speak with authority, opening the little book to Article 24 of the Constitution, and reading about religious rights. *"Every person has the right to the freedom of convictions of ethics, of conscience, and of religion, and to have or to adopt, as may be the case, that of his/her preference."*

The young man said, "You all know me - I'm from here. I'm a Catholic, like you all. I go to the witchdoctor when I'm sick. But let's be realistic. Mexico allows freedom of religion. It's in our Constitution. We can't stop people preaching. But - these people are foreigners." He spoke to Jason. "Do you have your papers?"

Jason did. He showed him his papers, allowing him to work as a missionary in Mexico. It was enough to solve that problem.

The man went on, reading slowly and clearly. "Here in Article 27, it says this: 'However, the decrees enacted under the situations described in the previous paragraph cannot restrict or suspend the exercise of the following rights: ... the freedom of ideas, conscience *and to profess any religious belief'* ..."

The man finished reading and speaking. He let the words sink in. And, amazingly, the people paid attention to what he said. Slowly, they began to lower their weapons. Then they turned and walked away. All except Joaquín and his family, who stayed to hear about Jesus and give their lives to Him.

It took a long time, but 13 years later we celebrated the successful inauguration of a small, roofed, church meeting area in Zempoala. Brother Joaquín, at the age of 72, was in tears as he shared his story of how God had touched his life as a child through others' evangelistic efforts, then he responded to the same gospel message, preached by Jason, in 2004!

The persecution and threats are still there, but we serve a big God who does big miracles!

* * *

During these times, while Jason was traveling and sharing the gospel, I was mainly at home in Tenango de las Flores. Right away I started a ministry to unwed mothers, taking them into my home to minister to them and their children. These were mostly young women in very difficult circumstances - some of them had been victims of rape, some were orphaned and grieving. They had to fend for themselves and try to provide for their children with no support from anyone. Proportionally, there were so many more unwed mothers in Tenango and the surrounding villages than in Xochiatipan - the percentage in that county was much higher.

I also began to notice the needs of the children around us. Small children would often come knocking and ask me to give them work - not money, or food, but work, so that they could eat.

"Señora Nicole, can I cut your grass?"

"Would you like me to water your plants?"

"Señora Nicole, can I walk your dogs?"

I wanted to increase what I could do for the children. I talked to our ministry leaders, and they agreed that this was an important ministry. So, in March 2004, we moved into a much bigger, two-storey four-bedroom house in the same town. It was on a hill, with a direct view of the calm, picturesque Tenango lake and the tree-filled mountains beyond. Guess what was right in front of the house? A huge magnolia tree, in full bloom!

In this new, beautiful house, I gave the little kids small yard jobs to do, a healthy meal, some cake and milky coffee. I started a mini-refuge for the kids who lived on the street, or who had nothing to eat or wear. I opened up a type of school that gave Bible and reading classes to the children, helping them learn to read and write. Many of them didn't go to any school at all; they were just too poor. I used material developed in Cuba called *"Yo, Sí Puedo"* (Yes, I Can) that has been very successful in teaching children and adults to read and write. Within the first year, we'd gone from just a few kids to 40.

During this time, God connected us to Dr. Antonio Morales and his precious wife Margarita, a strong Christian couple who lived in the nearby town of Huauchinango. Not only did Dr. Morales look after me and my family, but he made it clear to us that he would look after anyone from the indigenous house churches we'd planted. And he did - we brought at least a dozen patients each week from the mountainous regions, and Dr. Morales tended to them all, including medicines and surgeries, *free of charge*. This was such an enormous help and blessing to us!

Just as we were settling into a good rhythm as a family in this new town, ministering to villages and women and children, we had an attack from the enemy ... and Jason almost died.

It was February 28, 2004, six days after those first wonderful baptisms in Caxapotla. Sed and Jasmine washed their Dad's motorcycle while Jason got ready to go visit a village called Tlapitzalapa, far away in the mountains, where he was in the early stages of starting a small house church. The road was a steep dirt track, filled with hairpin curves.

There were so many twists and turns, one after another. Jason took one curve a little too fast, lost control and was thrown off the motorcycle. He flew off the side of the road, down a steep cliff, through the bushes into a valley - landing hard in poison ivy, breaking his femur and his collarbone, and dislocating his knee!

There he lay, alone and in pain at the bottom of the cliff for a long time, until a government truck full of men coming back from work noticed his motorcycle lying at the edge of the road. They got out to see what had happened and called out. Jason called back for help. Thank God he was conscious when they came past, and able to yell up to them. They went down with some blankets, wrapped him up and dragged him all the way back up the steep hill. It wasn't easy - apart from being careful with his fractures, Jason was tall, muscular and heavy. It was quite a feat to get him up 30 feet (9 meters) to their vehicle to take him to safety.

* * *

Our small, very rustic satellite phone rang and I answered it. "Do you know a ... Haso Escot Fispadri?" I heard a man ask. I got over my initial confusion and said "Yes". My body went cold as the man proceeded to tell me what had happened. *Jason in an accident? At the bottom of a cliff? Couldn't move?* I had no idea how badly hurt he was.

My mind began to race. I had flashbacks to my own accident and time in the hospital. I called our ministry leaders in Texas, who immediately began making phone calls and radio messages. Our co-worker, Britt Hancock, just happened to be driving about 3-4 hours away from Jason, on his way back to Cuetzalan from Veracruz. He was in an area where there was no radio contact - yet somehow, miraculously, he heard the call on his radio. We all worked out a place for the three of us to meet, at a gas station about an hour away from our house.

I got a friend to help drive me and my kids out. As we traveled and I prayed on the way, I could see God's hand in bringing those workers to help Jason, and in having Britt be in the vicinity at just the right time. Just as we arrived at our rendezvous point, so did Britt (coming from the north) and the truckload full of Good Samaritans carrying Jason (from the southeast)!

There I saw my husband, pale and with welts from the poison ivy, shivering from shock and in agonizing pain, still wrapped in the blankets. He was in terrible shape, but thank God he was alive. He wasn't able to sit up in any vehicle, so the men put him into the back of Britt's truck. It was a small truck, and Jason was too long for the truck bed - they couldn't close the tailgate! Britt secured it as best he could. Jason had to lay in great pain on a plank of plywood in the back of the truck for another grueling 6 hours with his eight-year-old son sitting with him in the cold and holding onto his arm, while Britt drove us all slowly down the bumpy roads to a hospital. Jasmine sat in the front between Britt and I, on her knees, looking out the back window at her father and brother for the entire trip.

Jason was immobile for several days as he waited for blood transfusions. We didn't know it until then, but he has O-negative blood; it's a rare blood type, but always in demand in emergency situations due to its versatility for all patients. At first at the hospital I was handed a styrofoam cooler and told to "go find blood". Britt drove me around Tampico, Veracruz, trying to find the blood, to no avail.

It took a long time for the hospital to find blood. They had to make radio announcements in other states; and when they finally found some - in Monterrey - a volunteer took an overnight bus all the way to the hospital to get it to us as soon as possible. Jason had major surgery on his femur and knee. He was released a week later, but confined to home and unable to walk for months.

We could see God's hand in saving Jason's life, sending those men to help, using Britt at just the right time, and getting the blood he needed. Yet it still felt like a great blow to all that we were trying to achieve in Tenango. We had to keep trusting the Lord that the move we'd made had been the right one. In between nursing Jason and homeschooling Sed and Jasmine, I continued taking in children as I saw their needs, helping them with food, clothing, and schooling.

And as I helped, God moved me in an unexpected direction.

CHAPTER TWELVE

The Crossroads

"But whoever causes one of these little ones who believe in Me to stumble, it would be better for him if a millstone were hung around his neck, and he were thrown into the sea." - Mark 9:42 (NKJV)

Hope has two beautiful daughters. Their names are anger and courage; anger at the way things are, and courage to see that they do not remain the way they are. - Augustine

THE BOOK OF Esther has always fascinated me. I love to read her story. A Jewish orphan who lived in Persia after many Jews had returned to the land of Israel, Hadassah was raised by her older cousin, Mordecai. He was a noble man who knew and feared God and had saved the life of King Ahasuerus from an attempted assassination.

Because the favor of the Lord was upon her, Hadassah became the King's wife - Queen Esther, she was named. It was a fairytale story, it seemed; until her own people, the Hebrews living under Persian rule, became the targets of a royal decree to annihilate them all, initiated by an ambitious, narcissistic man named Haman, and unwittingly signed by the King.

Would the Lord God allow His people to be entirely wiped out? His promises through the prophets of a coming Messiah indicated that surely this would not happen. But who could save them? There was only one person capable of going right to the top and speaking directly to the King: Queen Esther.

But the personal risk was enormous. Esther had to risk her life in appearing before the King. At first, she balked. The chance of being put to death was high for appearing unannounced and uninvited. But Mordecai helped her see the bigger picture.

And Mordecai told them to answer Esther: "Do not think in your heart that you will escape in the king's palace any more than all the other Jews. For if you remain completely silent at this time, relief and deliverance will arise for the Jews from another place, but you and your father's house will perish. Yet who knows whether you have come to the kingdom for such a time as this?"[9]

Esther rose to the occasion. She realized that God had placed her in a unique place, for the salvation of her people, even if it meant she perished.

* * *

The longer we were in Tenango de las Flores, the more I began to notice a number of differences between the children of this town and the ones from Xochiatipan. The little ones here were utterly impoverished. There was a deep, silent darkness that surrounded them: they were filthy, and there were signs of appalling neglect.

I'd ask them where their parents were, and they'd say all sorts of things to me: *he's in the field working ... she's taking care of my sick grandma ... in the city helping my aunt who just had a baby*

---

9. Esther 4:13-14, NKJV

... None of the children attended school; most had no idea what their last names were, or when they were born.

As the months passed, I saw problematic signs on many children: black eyes, bite marks, burns, cuts, bruises, swollen legs. I began to wonder what all this was about. I'd ask the children what had happened to them; they'd look down and reply that they were bitten by a neighbor's dog, that they'd tripped, that they'd fallen out of a tree, that they'd been clumsy and knocked over some hot water. It seemed unlikely that all of these stories could be true, but I was naive and I truly wanted to believe them.

I'd clean up their wounds and put bandaids or ointment on them to help them heal. I hoped that if they weren't telling me the truth, that one day I'd earn their trust enough for them to tell me what had actually happened. But I knew something definitely wasn't right.

This continued until two young sisters who'd often come to my house began to fall asleep during the classes. Keila was 11 and Laura was 13, yet they were the same height, with sad eyes, their expression often cast downwards. They hardly spoke and would not eat anything, saying that they felt a little nauseous. I was pretty sure it was stomach and intestinal parasites, because they obviously came from a very poor background and had never had any vaccinations or seen a doctor before. It was a common enough occurrence. I took them to a local clinic so that the doctor could prescribe them some de-worming medicine.

I sat on a blue plastic seat in the small office, looking at the doctor's degrees framed on the walls and trying to locate him in the picture of his graduation class with 50 other medical students all dressed in white, while he examined the two little girls. I was mildly surprised he was taking such a long time just to diagnose parasites. Then the doctor looked up at me gravely. "These girls are both pregnant," he said to me.

I jumped in my seat. That was not a word I was expecting to hear. *Pregnant*? Surely it wasn't possible - *how* could they be pregnant? They were just children! Was this even physically possible? The doctor noticed my expression, and tried to reassure me. "This is quite normal, Señora. These are indigenous girls; they obviously live in poverty. Incest is very common among these people. The rape of little children is normal around here."

Upset, I gathered the girls together and took them outside. I was bewildered, filled with unbelief. More proof was required. I decided to take them to get blood tests done. It took an hour to get the results; an hour of restless waiting and wondering. The blood tests confirmed it: these two underdeveloped, sickly, bruised, illiterate girls were both pregnant!

As I drove home with the girls, I began to feel cold and shivery. My mind whirled with questions. I didn't want to ask them - but I had to. Surely for their sake I had to ask them! I had to find out! But - what might I find out? Was it molestation? Incest? Abuse? Who had raped them?

My mind reeled at these words that were not part of my normal vocabulary and the implications they carried. Wouldn't it be a lot easier to simply carry on as before, sending the girls away with food and clothes, hugs and prayers, and saying nothing? But - what about all those other children who came to my house? Maybe they were being abused too - and I didn't want to see it.

I realized I was at a crossroads. And the decision I was about to make - whether to conclude I couldn't do anything about it and turn away sadly, or whether to step up and do something about this situation - was going to determine what I'd do every time I was faced with another abused child.

Arriving home, I made up some beds for Keila and Laura, and waited until the two girls along with Sed and Jasmine were asleep. Then I told Jason all about our trip to the doctor and what he had said. Jason was sitting in the living room, his broken leg raised and resting on a cushion. As I repeated the doctor's words out loud, my face grew hot with shame and my voice trembled. Jason's face grew very serious. "What are you gonna do about it, Nicole?" he asked.

I looked at him squarely. "I'm going to help them, J. I can't turn them away. I've gotta look after them." I had no idea what this might mean, but I knew I would not turn back.

Jason agreed with me. "Well, you know I'll support you if you think it's what you should do," he said. We prayed about it together, earnestly asking the Lord for wisdom and guidance. And we decided something needed to be done; and if no-one was doing anything, maybe God had put us in that place - in Tenango de las Flores - to fill that gap.

I asked the questions that needed to be asked. And I found out the answers, difficult as it was to hear them.

First, I spoke to the two little girls after a meal. I sat them down and spoke to them very calmly. "Keila and Laura, I love you both very much. I'm not mad, or angry, and I'm not rejecting you at all. What happened to you was not your fault. You are both innocent - you are victims." The girls were calm, but looked a little uneasy as to where I might be heading with an introduction like that. "Do you understand that you're both pregnant?"

They looked at me blankly. I might as well have asked them if they could recite to me the book of Isaiah from memory.

I considered my resources. I got up and went to my library, returning with a book on the human body and another one called "*Where There Is No Doctor*". I showed them pictures of the bodies of a boy and a girl and asked them, "Have you had sex with anyone?"

Again, the blank looks. "What's that?" Laura asked.

I had to become even more specific, and explain to them exactly what sex was. I felt embarrassed to do it with such young girls. But finally they understood. "Oh, yeah," Laura said, nodding, "I've done that since I was little."

I wasn't sure she had really understood, but she went on. "My older brother started coming into our room and he'd do that to me. He told me not to tell anyone. It was a secret. Then he started doing it to Keila as well."

The girls both began to open up to me, and told me their story - and I asked neighbors and did my own investigation. When Keila and Laura were very small, about 2 and 5 years old, their mother abandoned them, leaving them in the "care" of their father and his new wife - their stepmother - in a tiny, decrepit wooden shack with empty bottles and garbage on the ground. Their father was a known alcoholic, often lying in filthy clothes passed out in the streets. The stepmother was cruel to the girls, abusing them mercilessly, telling them they were good for nothing.

Then their older brother, who was about 16, began to abuse them sexually. He brought his cousins to the shack, where they'd watch porn and then act out what they'd seen on their two little cousins. Later he began to rent his sisters to others - each and every night - old men and young, alcoholics and drug addicts, for just a few dollars apiece.

The girls looked so small and vulnerable as they shared all this with me. "Did you ever try to make them stop?" I asked them.

"I wanted to," answered Keila, "but my brother told me to close my eyes and just take it." Her face brightened up. "And afterwards he'd buy us a piece of chocolate or a steak taco, or sometimes some new clothes!"

I felt sickened, and disgusted at humanity. How could anyone use little children like this? I thought of my own beautiful children, how they'd blossomed and thrived as they received all my love and care throughout their childhood. It was heartbreaking to think of these two little girls who had received only unkindness, treachery and abuse of the worst kind from those who were supposed to care for them; being taken advantage of daily with no way to stop it ... And now these children were expecting babies of their own.

I decided to fight on behalf of Keila and Laura. I went directly to the police in Tenango and told them about the two little girls. The officials looked at me with an amused expression - what did this *gringa loca* think she was going to achieve? Besides, they had hundreds of cases. They didn't need two more.

I contacted a personal friend who was an attorney. He told me that as a foreigner, I needed to be very careful. I couldn't directly press charges on their behalf. He began to speak directly to authorities for us. He spoke to the town president, and managed to get a case file opened for both sisters. I began to find out how I could legally get those girls out of their desperate situation, and with God's help I got them out. The girls found safety at our house and with my family, living with us during their final months of pregnancy, and I helped them give birth to their beautiful children - a girl and a boy.

I didn't stop at rescuing the girls, either; with the help of my lawyers I went after their abusers to make sure they couldn't do this to any other human being. The brother escaped, but the father was sentenced and jailed. The heinous sin committed against Keila and Laura had a name.

Child sex trafficking.

I'd heard of sex trafficking before; I'd seen movies on it. But I had not the slightest idea how common it really was, or how it was viewed in many areas of Mexico - that for many, molesting girls from their own family was perfectly normal, something the girls had to grow up with as part of their family's context.

In some towns it was generational - grandmothers and mothers would often tell their daughters they had to hush and obey, just as they'd had to do when they were young.

In the same way, men paying to sleep with young women and children was considered a normal part of life - unpleasant perhaps for the girls, but normal nonetheless. In these places, many teenage boys had grown up believing that life consisted solely in fulfilling their personal desires - especially in drinking and having sex; and that the more they had of both, the bigger "men" they would be - the more they could boast with their friends. Men did not work for their families; they didn't want to work at all, only enough to buy a cell phone and watch pornographic videos. And many women were complicit in allowing the men these excesses, some even benefiting financially from them in providing the young girls for their pleasure.

How could anything so heinous be considered as normal as buying candy at the store? My mind could not fathom it.

I learned that, incredibly, there is an entire town in Mexico called Tenancingo which famously lives off the "industry" of human trafficking, with a full 10% of the population *actively* involved either as pimps, recruiters or as sex workers, and many more living and working with the knowledge that these activities exist on the same street.

If people in towns like Tenancingo and Tenango de las Flores actually thought about it they would admit that yes, it probably was evil, yet it was so prevalent that no-one could do or say anything about it. The more I looked into it, the more horrendous it was, and the angrier I became. Yet, as I looked around, nobody seemed to be doing anything about it; not to stop it, nor to rescue the children from these hellish lives.

I began to focus more on this work. We started to take in more girls - and also boys - who had suffered sexual abuse. We always worked with our lawyers, and began to get to know the ins and outs of the institution responsible for child and family welfare (known as the "DIF"[6]), in order to work alongside them and provide a safe place where children could be taken while their cases were being investigated and worked out. We took care of the children as best we could in our own house, giving them food, bathing them, giving them new and clean clothes, and helping them feel safe and protected.

My husband and I began to read and learn more, to make contact with international groups, and to raise awareness, speaking out against the atrocities of human (and specifically sex) trafficking. We learned that there are 250,000 children and adolescents trapped in sexual slavery - *in Mexico alone*. We discovered that 88% of trafficked children are actually sold out by someone from their very home - their father or mother, the boyfriend of their mother, or a stepfather, a brother, aunt or uncle, or even their grandparents.[7]

At first, many people we spoke to in Mexico didn't want to hear or think about sex trafficking or to admit that it existed. But the more we spoke, the more people began to come forward, timidly, sharing stories of children that they knew of: a family member who was being abused; a neighbor's young daughter who'd gotten pregnant; a classmate of their own children who had stopped going to school. A girl down the street who never left the house and whom men would "visit" during the day. They didn't really like to admit it or acknowledge it, but it was a weight off their chest that they could talk to someone who was actually willing to do something about it.

My lawyers and I investigated every case. We began rescuing children who were being rented out to a dozen men - or even more - each and every day. We also sought out and found children who were vulnerable because they'd been abandoned or orphaned; we took them in before any evil person could get their hands on them.

I once saw the movie *Robots*: in it, one of the main characters says, "See a need, fill a need!" When I heard that, it clicked with me - that's what we were doing, in an area where nobody was doing anything at all.

If you look up the dictionary definition of *human trafficking*, it says it is "an organized criminal activity in which human beings are treated as possessions to be controlled and exploited (as by being forced into prostitution or involuntary labor)".[8]

But our definition included the faces of the hurting little children we knew personally, who were being sold, rented, or exploited. Alone. Abused. Broken. Betrayed. Afraid. Desperately wanting love. A child's survival rate, when living on the streets, is very low without a miracle and some form of intervention. Words cannot express how this revelation impacted us. Our lives changed forever. Our eyes were opened.

We realized that God had prepared us - and especially me - for such a time as this.

CHAPTER THIRTEEN

Mamá Nicole

Rescue those who are being taken away to death, And those who are staggering to the slaughter, Oh hold them back! If you say, "See, we did not know this," Does He who weighs the hearts not consider it? And does He who watches over your soul not know it? And will He not repay a person according to his work? - Proverbs 24:11-12 (NASB)

To live our lives and miss that great purpose we were designed to accomplish is truly a sin. It is inconceivable that we could be bored in a world with so much wrong to tackle, so much ignorance to reach and so much misery we could alleviate. - William Wilberforce

FROM THAT FIRST case in 2004 and over the next few years, this ministry to children - rescuing them from the streets, child sex trafficking, exploitation, abandonment or abusive environments and giving them a safe place to stay - began to flourish.

Although our house overlooking the lake in Tenango was large, the needs began to outgrow our space. More and more children arrived - malnourished, impoverished, traumatized, abused and neglected - and within a few years two things became increasingly obvious. The first was that this was truly my calling from God: this was what He had prepared me to do, and I was ready to make it my mission for life. The second was that we needed to find a bigger space, one that could allow us to properly expand and rescue many more children.

In 2007, we started the search for land; somewhere that could be developed into a community where children could not only be safe, but could receive healing and begin to thrive. The Lord did a wonderful thing. He led us to 6.6 acres (2.7 hectares) of land in the same area where Jason had celebrated his first baptism and started his first house church after we moved to Tenango de las Flores - outside a small village called La Gallera, just a short drive from Tenango.

It took an enormous amount of sacrifice on our part, but in 2008 we signed the papers and began the process of building and moving into what would soon become *Casa Hogar La Aldea* (Village Children's Home, or VCH). This name represented community, a small place like a village in which the children could grow, flourish and be family.

It was a huge block of land, 4600 ft² (1400 m²) up on the side of a lush mountain, with a breathtaking view of forests and hills, and a river running through it. Cool, fresh air. Sounds of peace and nature: the wind in trees, the birds - including toucans and parrots. It was close to town, but not in the town, which gave us more security. The only setback was the rain. In this region it rains 8-10 months of the year, preventing the normal two crops per year that much of Mexico gets, and creating mold and mildew a lot more quickly. The people of the area grow and sell ornamental flowers and trees, along with coffee. The damp, sweet coffee smell permeates the entire region.

The early years of the Village can be described in one word:

rustic! It was just Jason and me with Sed and Jasmine - and up to 40 children. There was no electricity: no fridge or freezer, no light at night. We showered using buckets. The toilets were primitive outhouses. We washed all our clothes by hand; I'd get up very early in the morning each day - around 4 am - and hand wash as many clothes as I could before waking everyone up at 5am; everyone had to be in the dining room/prayer room at 5:30 am.

The buildings were a series of wooden cabins set on cement foundations and with exposed wooden rafters. We used every ounce of space for necessary items, creating little upstairs lofts for storage and other bedrooms. In the biggest cabin we'd gather around the large table with all the children to read Bible stories and eat and play games. I tried hard to make each space pleasant and homelike, with flowering plants at the front door, pictures on the wall, light-colored curtains on the windows, candles and cushions.

During those years, leveling and building were constant, construction workers coming in and out, sounds of banging and the scraping of shovels scooping and mixing cement; there were slippery paths in the rainy season and muddy areas that came up to our knees. The first major construction we built was a pavilion: an awesome building with a kitchen, pantry, meeting area and dining hall.

All our food was made with fresh ingredients. Again, I felt like a missionary from the 19th century, bottling jam, pickling fruit and creating salsas from scratch. In order to cook, we created a cement fire pit on which we'd place a large heavy cast iron griddle known as a *comal* and gently heat freshly handmade corn tortillas. The warm fire was a favorite place for children with cold hands. We ate a lot of soups, noodles, rice, beans and lentils, with eggs for variety, as well as fruit and vegetables.

Sometimes people would ask me, "How on earth do you

feed and look after so many children at once? I struggle with two!" It was just a matter of keeping a routine, order, and consistent discipline. And feeding everyone was "What works for one, works for two, and works for 40". That said, cooking and cleaning involved creating systems that could handle lots of people: scheduled chores so that all the children participated in working together and keeping occupied.

Not only did we take in children. We also continued to care for unwed mothers; and at times we had elderly people who'd been abandoned by their family because they "couldn't care for them" - they were too old, "too much work". Some of them came from states as far away as Chiapas and Oaxaca in the south, and prosperous Nuevo León and Tamaulipas in the north - driven up to the mountains by their family and simply left there. Unwanted. We'd find elderly men and women living on the streets, impoverished and dying.

I was appalled, and unable to leave them in this condition. God's heart for the destitute and abandoned reaches also to those nearing the end of their lives. We'd take them in, bathe them, trim their hair and nails, tend to their medical needs, and look after them in their final days, showing them who Jesus is. They'd become family - we called them the Village *abuelos* (grandparents) - and they'd stay with us until Jesus called them home.

I homeschooled all the kids throughout each week. And for years, every single Saturday we sent our trucks to the surrounding house churches in order to bring the children to the VCH for Children's Church, which went for the whole day. The place would be packed! I'd spend the entire week finding fun songs, stories, games, and crafts ready for the kids, and bake hundreds of cookies on Friday. I'd feed them all and teach them the Word of God. The kids were fascinated by the Flannelgraph Bible stories with cutout figures that I would stick onto a large illustrated panel. It was so much fun - and with so many kids on hand it wasn't too much work; I always had helpers.

At this point, you may be wondering about my own children. I've often been asked how my "biological children" were able to adapt to having so many other children around, all needing my attention and care. The truth is, Sed and Jasmine were always supportive of us helping children. They were never against it; on the contrary, they were - and still are - our biggest fans. Their hearts held the same compassion for rescuing and taking care of destitute children. And I love to see how the other children honor Sed and Jasmine. There is nothing that gives me greater joy than having my son and daughter close by and knowing they are fully behind what we do.

As the years passed, however, Jason and I realized that we did need space and time as a family. We tried hard to keep each Wednesday as "Family Day" in which the four of us could go out and eat a meal and create special moments together. It didn't always go as planned, but we tried. And we made a lot of wonderful memories with Sed and Jasmine.

In the midst of all the routines and activities were the constant reminders that the children living with us at the VCH were not on some special summer vacation from their own wonderful home environment. These were children who'd been betrayed, used, traumatized by the people who were supposed to be their most loving carers.

In a way, it's strange to think that although our wooden cabins at the Village in those early years were so rustic and basic, they were palaces compared to where the children had been taken from: brothels, street corners, even - literally - trash pits. They arrived at the Village feeling insecure and frightened, with the hurt showing in their eyes; often with bruises and cuts, with lice crawling in their matted hair and dirt ingrained in every pore of their dry skin. They'd nervously fiddle with their hands and fingers and silently avoid any eye contact. Their first nights would be filled with nightmares and tears - and bedwetting, even for teenagers. There would be moments of inexplicable outbursts, triggered by a smell, a sound, a word, which unknown to us carried with it a memory too painful to express.

There were endless court cases; they were (and still are) so terribly draining and unpleasant. It's an awful thing to make a child have to recount and relive in their minds what was done to them in front of others. Thankfully a court hearing in Puebla is not like what we often see on TV shows. I'm sitting in the courtroom just a few meters from the perpetrator; I have to testify against them and they against me. Both prosecuting and defense attorneys ask us questions.

But the child is not in that courtroom - he/she is in a different room, with their psychologist and district attorney making sure they're comfortable and calm, with snacks, so he/she can answer the questions via livestream video without being able to see the people in the courtroom. But there are so many questions. It's very uncomfortable, and always a relief when it's over and we can go get an ice cream or a milkshake.

* * *

People who supported us from the USA and sometimes visited us would ask me, "How would you describe what you are doing for these children, Nicole?" I realized there were three actions I was consistently carrying out in order to help the children, and continue to do: **rescue, restore,** and **raise.**

You might think the word *"rescue"* sounds heroic and exotic. Well, the team of people I have now are truly heroic. But there is nothing exotic about the reality of where these children are often rescued from.

Rescuing the children sometimes includes entering brothels. Some of these are entire hotels/motels, or apartments with rooms and beds separated by sheets, but often in the small towns they are small wooden huts of 10 x 15 ft (3 x 4.5 m) with small beds also separated by a sheet where little girls would be rented to men by family members - including grandparents. The rooms are dark, the beds filthy, and the children are often unbathed and hungry.

But rescuing also happens at traffic lights and street corners, where children are exploited by adults to sell sweets or wash windshields. A number of our rescues are not only from sex trafficking, but from human trafficking and exploitation in general, such as kids working in sweatshops or street stands. It's so often the case that the two crimes go hand in hand - adults exploiting the children by day by making them work, and at night raping them or renting their bodies to strangers.

There are different ways we go about these rescues. It can be by word of mouth, or a tipoff from someone working in crime prevention; or because a concerned neighbor or family member calls the police or the DIF to report possible child abuse; or when we see with our own eyes a child who is in a vulnerable state.

But the rescues are neither quick nor easy. They take a lot of investigation, preparation, and coordination in order to make sure everything is done according to the law and with the child's well-being as top priority.

* * *

What comes after the rescue? Restoration. We work hard to *restore* every child physically, emotionally, mentally, and spiritually.

I restore the children's bodies by getting rid of worms, parasites and lice, and treating them for STDs. I give them good food, bathe them daily, cut their hair, buy them new clothes and shoes, and paint the girls' fingernails. We take them to the doctor and the dentist. The children have a chance to feel clean, healthy and free. I hold them and help them feel safe with loving, unthreatening hugs and kisses.

I have to restore them emotionally, giving many a childhood they never had. Back in those early years, I was on my own, doing the best I could as I held the children tight while they wept on my shoulder, and stayed up with them at night as they detoxed or couldn't sleep because of nightmares. I let them be kids again: playing hide and seek, chase, and musical chairs. I'd rock the babies while their young mothers would jump on the trampoline screaming and laughing like toddlers. I'd tell each one daily how much I loved them.

The children also need to be restored mentally. Dignity and self esteem are the first things that are harmed when a child suffers physical and/or sexual abuse. I thank God daily for the full-time Christian professional psychologists and psychiatrists He has provided who share this burden with me and give the children a chance to heal what is torn and broken inside. We have to be careful to avoid re-victimizing the children. Not only do we put them through therapy, but we steer them forward to a better future. We give them ways to think differently about themselves, and help them to create good habits and make positive decisions so that their minds can be healed.

And finally, the children are given the chance to know and put their trust in our Creator God and King, and Jesus our Redeemer and Rescuer. They are restored spiritually through worship, listening to Bible stories, memorizing Scripture, being prayed for and praying for others, as well as through counseling, mentoring and discipleship.

Restoring the children takes time. The road to restoration is hard and super bumpy. At times they lash out and reject the ones who love them most. They test us. They want to be sure we can be trusted. But when it's all said and done, it is so very worth it.

Then, if possible we reintegrate them to a safe, distant family member who either knew nothing of the abuse or were the ones who reported it to me and helped me rescue them. They need to be trustworthy and willing to take in the children as if they were their own.

At the beginning, if the parent in charge of the child was struggling with addiction to alcohol or drugs, we would give them the chance to go through rehabilitation and help them financially. Back then, I was naive about many things. I didn't realize that a lot of the parents were themselves damaged from their own traumatic childhood. They were unable to release their minds and hearts from the habits and thought patterns that had shaped their entire lives.

Even - and I do not say this lightly - even when they received Jesus as their *Savior*, it was not enough, unless they also understood and accepted Jesus as *Lord*, allowing Him to begin the often painful process of transforming them from the inside out. There were those who accepted Jesus and even evangelized others, and still raped or rented their little daughters at night. We cannot even begin to understand this mentality and these atrocious acts, contradicting what Jesus came to save us from. These generational curses need to be broken through confession and repentance, so that they will no longer be repeated and their cultural thought-patterns and practices can be replaced by godly obedience in Jesus' name and for His sake.

This is why in later years we've focused a lot more on promoting foster care and adoption, as many families are simply unable to care for their children in appropriate ways. But it's wonderful when we can find a loving, reliable family member who is keen to give the child a chance to start again.

As the children are restored in all these ways, the opportunities they have for a life and future with dignity begin to open up in ways they could never have dreamed of. Many have attained college or technical degrees; some are married to national missionaries; some are now full-time staff members and help us care for others.

For me, this is huge! Can you consider how amazing it is that a child who was abandoned and abused, tortured and traumatized, forced to work or to perform sexual acts on older men day after day, can have their life restored to the point of becoming a healthy, happy, productive member of society who loves Jesus and wants to help others?

* * *

The third thing I would do for each child under my care (and still do) was to *raise* them. Some children were with me for a very short time, while their case was being completed or if there was a good solution that was readily available. But there were many others who simply had no-one to look after them, no-one to come for them or ask about them. And foster families and forever homes willing to adopt have only just recently begun to be promoted in Mexico as good and worthwhile options. So a lot of children have stayed with me and become truly my sons and daughters, right through their teen years and into study, work, and marriage.

Yes, I did whatever it took: buying school books and backpacks and taking them to school; providing medical attention whenever a boy fell and broke an arm; getting glasses for all the kids with poor eyesight; providing braces for all those kids with wonky teeth; soothing the tummy pains and calming the bickering among siblings. I attended to all their needs, just as if I was their Mom and they were my very own.

That's who I became - and still am, to this day. *Mamá Nicole.*

CHAPTER FOURTEEN

Trials and Faith

"Do not worry then, saying, 'What are we to eat?' or 'What are we to drink?' or 'What are we to wear for clothing?' For the Gentiles eagerly seek all these things; for your heavenly Father knows that you need all these things. But seek first His kingdom and His righteousness, and all these things will be provided to you. So do not worry about tomorrow; for tomorrow will worry about itself. Each day has enough trouble of its own." - Matthew 6:31-34

After the Lord has tried our faith, he, in the love of His heart, gives us an abundance. For the glory of His name and for trial of our faith, He allows us to be poor and then graciously supplies our needs. - George Müller

OVER THE YEARS that Jason and I have been in Mexico, we've seen and experienced a lot of miracles. Apart from the miracle of seeing people come spiritually alive when they put their trust in Jesus, God has multiplied food, healed many different diseases and health issues, and even raised people physically from the dead.

But one big miracle keeps coming back to me. It was the day before the *Día de los Niños* (Children's Day, April 30th). Children's Day in Mexico is a big thing - schools and shopping malls hold special events, neighbors gather the kids together on the street and break open piñatas, toys and candies are given out. It's a day to make every child feel special.

I had promised the kids at VCH that we would do something, as we always did - usually we had a big pizza, hot dogs, or hamburgers, along with a piñata. Every couple of days the kids would ask me, "What are we going to do for Children's Day?" And I'd answer, "It's a surprise."

I said this because I wasn't sure just how much money would come in. The week before that particular Children's Day we had a lot of big medical expenses for a number of people from our house churches. Someone needed emergency surgery; another was having an emergency C-section; it was one expense after the other, and we paid for all the bills with everything in our bank account. Back then, about 10 years ago, we'd only get one deposit a week for our support. So until that deposit came through, we were down pretty low on finances.

That entire week before Children's Day, and as a result of all the extra expenses, we also lived on lesser amounts of food, using up what we had in our pantry - beans, rice, lentils. It wasn't a problem, I thought. I fully expected money to come through the following week.

So on April 29th I drove up to Huauchinango to check how much money had come in and to get money out of the bank. My plan was to withdraw the money, go buy the food and the piñata for Children's Day, and come back to VCH.

But when I put my bank card into the ATM and requested money, it refused. That was weird, I thought. I did a quick balance inquiry, and stared with shock at the amount the ATM showed me. We had about $2 in our account.

Now this was not the first time we'd had a low amount in our bank account. But it was the day before a special occasion for the kids. I had 60 excited kids! My heart sank to the ground. I felt I was letting them all down. I was devastated, and heartbroken.

At the same time, I had faith that God could - and would - do something. I thought of George Müller, that amazing Christian man who cared for thousands of orphans in West England, and who never asked for a single penny, firmly believing that God would always provide for all the children's needs. Not a day went past when the children did not eat. And yet there were moments of trial, such as the time when there was no food for breakfast, and yet Müller prayed and thanked God for His provision. There was a knock at the door - it was the local baker, who in a dream had been told to bake enough bread for all the orphanage children for a week. And right behind him was the milkman, whose truck had broken down, and rather than letting the milk spoil while he made repairs, he donated all the milk to Müller's orphanage.

I knew of these stories. They've always inspired me. And I knew that Jesus Christ is the same yesterday, today, and forever[10] - He has not changed. I knew that God had told us to start the children's home, and that He'd said He would never forsake us. So I didn't freak out. I prayed, "God, I need You to come through somehow for the children. I trust You to do it."

I got back into the van and headed back to VCH. It was late in the afternoon now, April 29th. As usual, as I pulled up to the Village and parked the van, people ran out to greet me and to unload the van - ready to collect all the supplies and take everything to the pantry and kitchen. The adults and children looked inside, then looked at me in surprise and said, "There's nothing in the van!"

---

10. Hebrews 13:8

I said, "That's OK. Let's go down to the pavilion. Is supper ready?" It was.

My assistant walked up to me and spoke to me in a low voice. "You didn't get anything to eat?" she asked, bewildered.

"We didn't have any money come in," I replied.

She looked at me with growing concern. "Nicole," she replied, "We have *nothing* for the children to eat tomorrow. We have nothing to cook."

"What've we still got in the pantry?" I asked.

We checked together. There was one bag with about 4.5 lb (2 kg) of uncooked black beans. That was it. There was nothing else.

"What are we gonna do?" asked my assistant.

"We're going to get up in the morning and boil up those black beans," I answered. "We're going to trust God, and we're going to believe that we are in His will."

"What are we gonna tell the kids?"

"Nothing," I said firmly. "We are still going to celebrate Children's Day, any which way it happens."

The kids kept on asking me all that night, "What are we going to do tomorrow, Mamá Nicole? What are we going to eat for Children's Day?"

I repeated what I'd been saying to them for the last few days. "It's a surprise. You'll see."

Back in those days, we didn't have any internet at VCH. *We didn't even have electricity!* We couldn't jump on our cell phones and call someone for help, or send a quick SOS on Facebook. There was nothing we could do.

That night Jason and I prayed. "Lord, we know You called us to start this children's home. It's Children's Day tomorrow. We have nothing. If You want something to be done for the children, please do it."

The morning came. We had prayers as normal and Bible study, then the kids did their homeschooling tasks.

It was around lunchtime. There were 60-70 people to feed, and I had no idea what we were going to do. The ladies began reheating the cooked beans; all the while we were praying, "Jesus, please do something; we don't even have money for tortillas."

I was up at the buildings and heading down to the pavilion for lunch. I said to everyone, "We're just going to eat what we have."

At that moment I noticed movement on the road on the other side of the valley, leading towards the Village. There were two large new vehicles arriving. Big Suburbans. I turned and went to open the front gate. It was the brother of a longtime friend, along with his wife; they'd donated clothing and food before to VCH. This time they came with the owner of a big pizza parlor from Xicotepec, and with families from their kids' school. They'd wanted to bring a surprise for the kids for Children's Day - so they brought 40 or 50 large pizzas, chips, soda, plates, and 8 enormous piñatas filled with candies.

Everything that was needed for a huge celebration!

We all sat down to eat, giving thanks to God for the food. The children were so excited with the pizzas! We ate so much pizza. I have to say we absolutely stuffed ourselves full, and the pizzas just kept on coming! There were many pizzas left over after we'd finished.

After the pizzas the children went out and whacked those piñatas. They had a blast for a number of hours, playing and having fun with the school kids. It was wonderful to see their joy and hear their laughter.

And it doesn't end there.

When it was finally time for all these wonderful people to leave, we all walked up to the entrance of VCH to say goodbye.

While we were still hugging and thanking them, another vehicle turned up.

It was another big Suburban. A tall woman got out, in high heels and impeccably dressed, along with some helpers. She opened the back of the Suburban, and there was a massive 45 lb (20 kg) cake! It took about 8 guys to carry it carefully down to the pavilion. She also brought giant containers of homemade jello and other desserts. The timing could not have been better.

I did not even know who this woman was! She introduced herself. "My nephew, who is also my godson, came here a few years ago when he was about 16. At that time he was going through a rough time and you took him in and looked after him."

We remembered the boy. He was underage, so although he needed to be in rehab, he was not able to go to the men's drug and alcohol rehab center that Jason had recently established. So we took him in and helped him get off the drugs. He came from a well-to-do family from a city two states across from us. When he was better he returned to his family.

His aunt went on. "After he left the Village he was so much better. He went to high school, finished that, and now he's studying human rights at law school. He's doing great. We so appreciate what you did for him. We just wanted to come and say thank you and bless the children here on Children's Day." They'd driven about 6 hours with that massive cake, across two states, in order to bring that amazing blessing.

Of course, none of these wonderful people knew anything about what we were going through at the time.

By the end of the day, we were exhausted, full to the brim with food to spare, and totally blessed. So very grateful to God for what He did.

Some time later, during a children's church devotional time, I was sharing with the children on faith. I said how sometimes we pray and ask God for things we don't have, with faith that God will do it. I told them what faith is: "... the substance of things hoped for, the evidence of things not seen".[11] I shared with them the story of the day God came through for all the children. They were amazed - they had been partakers of a wondrous miracle.

Missionaries and many Christians are inspired by the great evangelical missionary history-makers. Their stories challenge and encourage us to step out in faith. We want to be great heroes, like them. But we don't generally pray and ask God for the trials that we have to go through in order to make us have that faith in God. Sometimes we get in His way, and stop His miracles for us, because in our own minds we can see no way, shape or form that it's going to happen.

Never doubt. Have faith. If God tells you to do something, you do it. He works in huge, mysterious ways.

---

11. Hebrews 11:1, NKJV

Chapter Fifteen

A Long and Hard Road

A father of the fatherless and a judge for the widows, is God in His holy dwelling. - Psalm 68:5

We have all eternity to celebrate the victories but only a few hours before sunset to win them. - Amy Carmichael

THEY WERE ONLY four and six years old when I first met them, and they'd already lived in hell. It took me seven years to rescue these two beautiful little girls. Seven long and painful years, the longest rescue I ever had to accomplish.

It was still in the early days at the Village. Jason had attended the funeral of an older man, a member of one of our house churches. Some of the sons and daughters of the man who had died had traveled a long way to attend the funeral. Jason came back from the funeral looking pensive, then he told me what was on his mind.

"I was talking with some of the sons and daughters of the

man who died," he said as he sat on the couch, his hands folded. "They were all pretty poor. When I told them what you do here at the Village, they pointed out to me two little nieces who were there with their mom and stepdad. They told me they think the little girls are being molested by their stepdad. Their father died before anyone had registered their birth, so when their mom got together with this other guy, he registered the two little girls in his own name, and now he's their legal father. They're just little girls, Nicole. If you'd seen them, I think you'd have suspected something too. What do you think we should do?"

"Call their mom," I replied. "Invite them over. They've come a long way for the funeral and they're poor. Tell them I have some gifts for her girls and I want them to come and have coffee with us."

The mom accepted the invitation, and arrived with her husband and the two little girls at our Village home. I greeted the four of them and brought them to our downstairs living room for the coffee that I'd promised. We introduced ourselves and I learned the mother's name was Juana, and the little girls were Nelly and Olivia. The girls were small and shy, not saying a word. As we sat down, I asked Jason in English to keep the mother and stepfather there chatting with him, while I took the girls upstairs for their gifts - brand new stuffed animals.

I brought the girls into my private counseling room, and gave them both a beautiful plush animal each. Their eyes lit up, and they hugged their new possessions tight. Then I spoke to the girls in a calm, gentle, reassuring voice.

"I want to ask you to be honest with me," I said to them both, but especially to Nelly, the older of the two. "Please tell me if anyone is doing bad things to you. No matter what you say, we will protect you and make sure they stop doing any harm to you."

It was not Nelly who spoke, but her four-year-old sister Olivia. She looked into my eyes and immediately began to share about how her older sister was treated. She told me in her own way that Nelly was being sexually assaulted, not only by their stepfather, but by the many men he brought into the house each day. She was being trafficked for sex every day, and she was six years old.

While Olivia was speaking, Nelly remained silent. She sat as still as a statue, staring into space. Suddenly, she began to sway back and forth. Her hands began to tremble as she grabbed handfuls of her hair and yanked hard; then her whole body began to shake. She was almost bouncing on her chair. I got up, stepped behind her, and leaned over her, taking her hands in mine, and embracing her tightly. As I held her tight she was able to slowly control her panic attack and calm the fear that had risen within her.

I sprang into action with my lawyers and therapists. We took the girls to press charges against their stepfather for pedophilia, sent the mother away, and gained custody of the two girls while we waited for the case to come to court. The judicial system in Mexico can take such a long time, especially when the mindset of so many people is that child sex trafficking is a normal part of life - there is no incentive for those within the system to move it forward. They don't always consider it worth their time or effort.

During the time the girls were with us, we gave them a safe place, food, clothing, warm hugs, and loving boundaries so that they could heal and learn to enjoy their childhood. They were sweet little girls - definite sisters, they looked so similar - and had begun to relax around me and give and receive hugs and kisses.

After about six months, Nelly and Olivia's mom came for them. She sat calmly and talked with me and said that she'd left her husband months ago and had reestablished herself in a different place, a nearby city called Poza Rica.

I listened to the woman speak. "I'm so much better now than before. I've left that awful man, and now I have a wonderful job in Poza Rica. I'm living with my brother - he's a Christian and goes to church and everything. I really think I can look after my girls again. I miss them so much, and I know I can do a better job now because I'm not in contact with my ex-husband anymore. Look - I'll give you my address in Poza Rica." She rummaged in her handbag for a piece of paper to write the address on.

I was of two minds as to what to do. I wished I could trust her, but something told me I shouldn't. I called my attorneys, who said that, as far as Mexican law is concerned, I had to give the girls back to their mother. But they reassured me that we would do an immediate follow-up of Nelly and Olivia in Poza Rica.

(I was not aware of it at the time, but Poza Rica is - to its shame - one of the biggest human trafficking centers of the world. Even way back in the 1930s, the burgeoning city - built on oil exploration by foreign companies - was the cradle of child prostitution as a means of fulfilling the foreign workers' "needs" without the messy consequences of unwanted pregnancies.)

A few days later, I went with my bodyguard and one of my attorneys to the address Juana had given me in Poza Rica. There was no-one there. The entire house was abandoned. I felt cold and hot, betrayed and angry. Not angry - furious. I became determined to rescue Nelly and Olivia.

And thus began the seven-year war for the lives of those two little girls.

* * *

Throughout this time I continued to rescue and raise many boys and girls - hundreds of other children - but I never stopped praying daily for those two dear girls and trying to find them. We were relentless. We covered about a dozen states, working with social justice systems in every state. I paid a lot of money for informants, private detectives, bodyguards, and police officers, to give me information. We did not stop. It cost me over $30,000 USD.

Then, out of the blue, I got a call from Juana. Nelly was with her, now 11 years old, but little nine-year-old Olivia had been kidnapped. That awful, perverted stepfather had taken her and disappeared.

It's a hard thing to write about, but for pedophiles, porn producers and sex traffickers, the younger the child, the better, when he or she is still underdeveloped and innocent. They wish to be the first to deflower the child. As Nelly began to grow older and show signs of puberty, her stepfather and the traffickers became less interested in her, and much more interested in her little sister ... and this made their mother very angry.

We find this all so difficult to understand. Why didn't the mother do something to stop all this the very first time it happened years ago? How could she allow these things to be done to her own children?

I drove with my attorney to locate Nelly first, according to the directions Juana had given us. We drove north, into the state of Veracruz, and picked her up as she came out of school in Poza Rica - in her dirty uniform, her stomach swollen with roundworms, unbathed, high on drugs. Her long, untied hair was crawling with lice. She had new scars and bruises on her little body. My attorney picked her up in his arms and she began to wail in fear, until she was able to register that I was there with her, and that she was now safe.

Immediately after rescuing Nelly we went to find her mother Juana, who signed the custody documents that very day so that we'd legally be allowed to take Nelly. We then made a bee-line to the Justice Department, and filed a kidnapping case against the pedophile stepfather. The mother signed the document with me.

* * *

It sounds unbelievable, but within a few months, we heard that Juana had moved in with a new boyfriend - who was actually an older cousin of Nelly and Olivia's - and that Olivia was back with them, but again being rented out to other men. The Justice Department had located Olivia and delivered her back to her mother, without convicting the perpetrator, and without contacting me, even though I was the one who'd pressed charges. The mother had simply switched from one evil man to another. And then they'd all disappeared. I was riled.

Every day we prayed for little Olivia, that we would be able to find her soon and bring her to the Children's Home. We searched and searched, hearing of leads and coming to dead ends. Each day seemed like an eternity for Nelly, who spent her time hoping, praying for news, and weeping silently.

Eighteen long months passed, and little Nelly was at breaking point. She felt that all the legal obstacles and her mother's stubborn refusal to change were making the search impossible. She decided it was time to take matters into her own hands.

It was September 16, 2016. We'd gone to a celebration of Mexico's Independence Day the night before at a church, and returned very late to the village. It was about 1 am in the morning when we finally got back with all the children. My staff forgot to lock the front gate. Nelly noticed this, and seized her chance to escape. She left VCH in the dark of the night.

I was devastated. She was putting herself at so much risk again, in order to find her sister and bring her back! We began the search for Nelly again as well, but to no avail. Yet God was in control of Nelly and Olivia's future.

Nelly had 50 pesos in her hand - the equivalent of about $2.50 USD. She took a 3-hour bus ride to Poza Rica, where she found the house of a cousin of hers. She asked her where her mother was. Her cousin made some phone calls, and told Nelly that her mom was in the city of Guadalajara, on the west side of Mexico. She gave her the address of the place where her mom could be found with her boyfriend and her daughter Olivia.

It was an extraordinary journey - one worthy of its own book one day. Nelly was now 13 years old but still little for her age; she valiantly set out, traveling from truck to bus, to another truck and another bus, and so on for two full days, all by herself, all the way to Guadalajara.

Nelly told me later that she was amazed at how much peace she had as she traveled. She would board a bus and the driver never asked her for money to pay her fare. They gave her the best seat on the bus, and they always left an empty seat next to her, as if there was an important-looking man sitting next to her accompanying her and paying for the entire trip.

It was truly a miracle that in Guadalajara - Mexico's second largest city - Nelly actually found the place where her little sister Olivia was being kept. It was a nondescript apartment building with a small sign which read "Massages for Gentlemen". Nelly stood outside the front for a minute, her heart beating hard. She knew what might happen if she entered. Then she walked up and opened the front door.

It didn't take long for her to locate Olivia in one of the rooms - along with her mom and her mom's boyfriend. Her mother jumped in surprise to see her. Poor Olivia was tied to the bed, her eyes terrified.

Nelly stepped forward into the room. "I've come for my sister," she announced bravely, with all the strength in her voice she could muster.

"You little *&^@! I'll make you miserable for all you've done to us!" the man growled. With two steps he was upon her. He grabbed her by the shoulder and re-broke a bone that had been fractured in the past. He brought Nelly to her knees. "You'll never get out of here!" he snarled. She could smell his alcoholic breath, and it almost made her sick. He grabbed her hands and she cried out in pain as he tied her up next to her sister in the bed. She wriggled and kicked desperately, as much as she could with the pain in her shoulder, but was overpowered.

Nelly was trapped with her sister and mother for 20 excruciating days.

Back at the Village, we continued to pray and search, using all the resources we could manage, to no avail. Then, out of the blue, on October 8th, I got a phone call. My heart leaped when I recognized the voice. It was Juana. Her words came out haltingly, as if she was unwilling to admit the truth, even after all she and her daughters had been through. "My daughters have finally convinced me that you can give us a better life. They want to go back to you."

I told her what to do. It took a couple of days, as she was under the control of this evil man acting as their pimp, and the only time she could do anything was when he left the brothel, or was too drunk or too high to notice. Juana went to a bank and opened a basic account that gave her a debit card so that I could transfer money to her.

On October 10, 2016, I got another call from her. "*Señora Nicole*," she said, breathing heavily into her cell phone as she ran and spoke at the same time. "I did it, we got out! We're going to the terminal! We're coming back!" They ran to the terminal, where I'd booked three bus tickets for them to take a bus to Mexico City, and they got on that bus to freedom.

At 2:30 the next morning, they arrived at Mexico City's northern bus terminal. My strong, capable husband, *Papá Jasón*, was standing there, waiting for them all as they stepped off the bus, tired, weak and pale, but safe at last.

October 11 is the International Day of the Girl Child. And on that very day Nelly and her sister finally escaped the hell they'd been put through.

Nelly and Olivia came back to the Village. They were given lots of love, time, and opportunity to heal, to study and dream of being social workers and psychologists, to love life and to receive God's sacrificial love for them, and to love Him back. To be baptized as followers of Jesus. Rented no longer - His forever.

I think back on those seven terribly long and difficult years and all the obstacles that came before us to stop us; on Nelly's fierce determination to find and free her sister; and on God's presence and grace with her, keeping her safe as she traveled and allowing her to convince her mother to find a way out. And I remember the Lord's words to me, back when I was lying in my hospital bed, lost and confused and wondering for what possible reason He had allowed me to live at all:

You have a very long and hard road ahead of you now. But I will be with you every step of the way. I promise.

CHAPTER SIXTEEN

The Shadow of His Wings

For, behold, the wicked bend the bow, They have set their arrow on the string To shoot in darkness at the upright in heart. - Psalm 11:2 (NASB)

Let us not look so much at who our enemies are as at who our Judge and Captain is, nor at what they threaten, but at what He promises. - Richard Sibbes

A WHILE BACK I was talking to a surgeon who'd been giving the children medical attention, and he was curious as to what I do. I began to share a little about the rescues, care, difficulties, etc. He looked at me for a while and said slowly, "This is a huge global problem. Why do you do this? What difference are you making besides these kids you have? Ma'am, they are going to catch up with you and *kill* you. It's not worth dying for. These are not your children."

I looked at him squarely and asked, "Do you have children?"

"Yes," he responded, "3 sons and a daughter."

I said, "What if it was your daughter they took?"

How quickly and straightly this tall, strong man sat up. His entire demeanor changed. He chose his words carefully but very decisively - including some graphic details. Suffice it to say, he would stop at nothing to rescue his daughter. I smiled and said, "Doc, I see every child as mine, and that is why I cannot stop."

* * *

I've always loved massively big dogs. Almost all my married life we've had Rhodesian Ridgebacks, Weimaraners, Belgium Shepherds, Boxers, and Rottweilers. But they're more than just my buddies. They're on guard 24/7, protecting us all. They sit or lie between the children and the adults, looking calm and peaceful, but they're always ready for any situation. They're also an amazing source of therapy for the kids. Gentle with the children, they endure a lot of "love torture" and patiently allow themselves to be played with as the children learn how to take care of an animal for the very first time.

There are a lot of firsts for the children in this ministry. Their first warm shower. Their first set of brand new clothes. Their first teddy bear. Their first home-made peanut butter cookies. The first time they can open up and share about what has happened to them. The first time they hear about the love of Father God for them. The first time they truly feel *safe*.

I have to say - it's incredible how many times people have set out to harm me or Jason - only to end up receiving God's justice instead. There was a man who decided to kill Jason for preaching the gospel out in the Nahuatl communities. That night, he was shot with his own revolver by an angry man in a bar.

There was another man who set out to do the same thing some time later - he was struck by lightning and killed.

I met a man once who was part of an infamous Mexican drug cartel, who told me that men from his cartel had been fixing to kill me - but that the night they were going to do it, men from another infamous Mexican drug cartel came and shot them all.

This has happened at least twenty times!

One Sunday night in December 2015 I was with a bunch of the older kids who'd joined me for an evangelistic Christmas campaign for children and families (which I do every year with the house churches and nearby towns). We'd just finished eating some hamburgers and were getting back into the vehicle in the nearby town of Nuevo Necaxa. I noticed some men in a car watching us ... but it was December, the town was busy with people everywhere, and I didn't think anything else of it. But alarm bells sounded in my head as we began to drive away and one of my helpers said to me, "Miss Nicole, I think that car is following us."

"Oh, no", I said. "You think so?"

We kept driving a little more. There was a lot of traffic on the road leaving the town, as we headed towards Xicotepec. My assistant grabbed my arm and with panic in her voice said again, "Miss Nicole! They're tailgating us! They're gonna hit us! It's those same people - I think they've got a gun!"

It was hard to shake them. But just before a bridge I managed to pull into a rest point at the very last second and the car was forced to pass us, surrounded by traffic. As it drove past I saw the AK-47s in the front held by men wearing masks. We'd recently rescued some girls from a drug gang; it seemed probable that this was a group from that gang. One of the teenage boys in our car carefully wrote down the license plate number of the car.

We stayed at that little rest point for a number of minutes. I was sure the car had turned left at the junction past the bridge, heading towards Mexico City. I pulled out and turned right at the junction - but to my dismay, just a little farther up the road, there they were, waiting for us. They pulled out right behind us, in between another car, and the chase was on again.

I prayed under my breath. I tried to maneuver a little, but with so many cars around it was hard to do. I called my lawyer, Armando, and put him on speaker phone; we gave him the license plate number, and listened to his careful instructions on how to shake them off our tail. We did just what Armando said, and managed it - and gunned the car down the highway straight to VCH. Later that night some of our male workers saw the same car driving past the large metal gates of our children's home.

The next morning I headed to Huauchinango, a town close to Tenango de las Flores for some court cases. At that time, my attorney Armando worked as a government councilor, in charge of the births and deaths of the district. He was looking through the records of incidents that had come through over the weekend. Then he stopped. I'd just walked into his office, and with a surprised expression he exclaimed, "Nicole!"

"What's going on?" I asked.

"Read me that license plate number you sent to me last night." I did, and he looked down again at the picture in front of him that had just been faxed in. "This is it - this is the car that was following you. I guess they were drinking, and they went off the edge." He showed me the picture: it was of a smoking, black wreck of a car, at the bottom of a cliff. It had gone off the side of a cliff and burst into flames. Everyone and everything inside the car - including their guns - was incinerated.

A Bible verse sprang to my mind. "*But if you truly obey his voice and do all that I say, then I will be an enemy to your enemies and an adversary to your adversaries.*"[12]

---

12. Exodus 23:22, NASB

* * *

Rescuing children has brought me into contact and cooperation with government agents and marshalls from Mexico, the USA, and further abroad. We usually have the support of the local police - even though I know for a fact that they've betrayed me and worked against me as spies during certain rescues. Sometimes they equip us with bulletproof vests and helmets; other times it's been a case of simply winging it as best we could in situations of life and death.

During rescues, there have been shots fired at us by the perpetrators - I've had a gun put to my head several times during intense moments of confrontation while trying to get children out of brothels or danger zones. Sometimes after rescues, we hear shots ringing out randomly nearby - gangs of narcos coming to scare us. Drug traffickers take pictures of us to intimidate us as we proceed with the rescues. They even try to press charges against me for removing the children from their clutches. Thankfully, many times the county authorities accompany me and use the law to help me.

There are also threats. At first, I received the occasional phone call or text message from a pimp or trafficker, telling me to return a girl or face the consequences. After a while, the threats became a daily occurrence. I had to hire a bodyguard to walk with me during the visits to the court and Ministry of Justice, because sometimes the threats were not empty - evil people really wanted me dead, and they paid people to make it happen.

One time, one night in May, my phone beeped at 3am, waking me with this message: "You *@&?#*$% dog! Why did you not give the phone to my daughters so they could wish me a happy Mother's Day yesterday?" *Seriously?!* This was sent to me by a woman whose daughters I'd rescued from the brothel where she'd been renting them to more than 15 men a day - and who had tried to have me killed more than once.

It's obvious that the Lord has protected us on multiple occasions - and these are just the ones I know about. I'm sure there are many more that went by us and we were unaware. This is not to say that we think we are invincible. But it's also unmistakable that God cares for the vulnerable, and He has kept us in the shadow of His wings[13] for almost 20 years, despite the attempts of the evil one to destroy us.

And he has helped me speak up for the children.

---

13. Psalm 63:7

CHAPTER SEVENTEEN

Be Their Voice

Open your mouth for the people who cannot speak, For the rights of all the unfortunate. - Proverbs 31:8 (NASB)

If to be feelingly alive to the sufferings of my fellow-creatures is to be a fanatic, I am one of the most incurable fanatics ever permitted to be at large. - William Wilberforce

"MAMÁ NICOLE, I don't want a cake for my birthday; I want your homemade cinnamon rolls, please!"

So I got up early this morning and made a huge bowl of dough to rise for Delia's birthday.

I returned home later than anticipated and exhausted after so many hours on bumpy roads dealing with rescue cases - but never too tired to bake. Delia was at my side the entire time as we rolled it out and saturated it with butter, sugar and cinnamon, but she hardly spoke a word.

Once we got them baked, iced and ready to serve, hot and soft like Delia had asked me, we surrounded her and sang happy birthday. And she stood there, with massive tears rolling down her cheeks.

It's too much at that moment. So new. So hoped for. So truly amazing. But they do not feel worthy: they feel angry and sad at the same time. Disoriented and confused. Reality gets mixed up with their sad memories and they don't know what to do with all the new feelings and emotions as the hot tears run down their faces.

* * *

Having a nuclear family is vitally important. It's the foundation that God gave us to establish strong bonds, an understanding of roles, a safe place to love and be loved. The Mexican Human Rights Commission also states that all children have the right to live in a family.[9]

But so many children globally are denied that right, due to war, drugs, abuse and abandonment - and human trafficking.

It's impossible to tell exactly how many children are being trafficked today, because so many cases are hidden from the public and not reported. According to UNICEF, 1 in 4 children under the age of 5 *don't even exist.*[10] How is this possible? It's because their birth was never registered. In small, impoverished communities, many people don't understand the importance of having an official identity, of registering their child with their own name.

Think about that for a moment. Imagine all the things we do in life that require that we show proof of identity and age! Going to school. Getting vaccinated. Going to the hospital. Getting our driver's license. Attending an event. Getting a job. Traveling overseas. Getting a bank account. The list goes on and on. People without a birth certificate cannot do any of these things. They are invisible to the government and to society in general.

And this makes them vulnerable: unknown and unidentified, they can be exploited in the worst possible ways. They generally can't read or write. If they attempt to migrate, there is no way of tracking them or checking their wellbeing. Nobody knows how to contact a family member if they get into some sort of trouble.

Human trafficking, and child sex trafficking in particular, is only getting worse. During the 2020 pandemic, sex trafficking increased in North America.[11] We are beginning to hear more about it as brave people speak up about the pedophile rings around the world that are covered up because of the rich and powerful who are involved and will do anything to keep up a front. But the majority of people do not want to hear about it. It's too horrific. They don't like it. It's better not to think about it.

Before I began to find out about human trafficking, I was completely unaware of those things happening around me. I could go anywhere and not see the signs of trafficking going on there, right under my nose. But all that has changed. I can't just sit and nod my head and enjoy the atmosphere anymore, because I know there is so much more to what's going on around me. I can't go back to the way I was before, at all.

I tried once. Jason and I went to Cancun. It was beautiful. But all the time we were there, I kept hearing Jason saying, "Nicole! Focus! You're here to enjoy yourself! Go down the beach and have fun!" It's because I was profiling every person I saw, and stopping every child on the street to see if they needed a home.

My sense of belonging has changed, too. In so many ways, I feel like I don't really fit in anywhere. I struggle a lot with this. I love my country; I'm a total patriot. But when I go to the USA now, I feel like I don't fit in with other women. For example, if I'm sitting at a pleasant restaurant with a group of nice ladies, sipping our teas, I'm looking around for predators. I'm looking for the bad guy. I'm going into the ladies' bathroom, looking at the feet under the stalls, listening for what I know to listen for, looking for what I know to look for. I would never have done before, and I know many have never thought about this, not even once.

I'll go back to the group of ladies and one of them will ask with a smile, "So, what do you do, Nicole? What is it that you do in Mexico?"

If I can, I try to get by with just answering with easy stuff. "Oh, I'm a missionary."

But people are often persistent. "What *exactly* do you do?"

"Well, we rescue children who've been abandoned or abused, or who are in poverty."

Then they'll ask more targeted questions. "Where do these children come from?"

It's at this point I have to begin telling them about human trafficking. And it's at this point that many of them start to feel awkward; some even freak out. For the most part, they don't want to hear it. I know that it makes them sad, scared, and un-comfortable. That is understandable. I do not know anyone who actually enjoys conversations about trafficking in children and what really goes on. The discomfort is greater if the women have children of the ages we deal with.

Almost without fail, the next response is, "But that's Mexi-co. That would never happen here in the US."

It's true, Mexico produces 60% of all the world's child por-nography[12] and is the number one country in the world for sex-ual abuse and trafficking in children[13]; and the atrocities I deal with in Mexico don't occur in the same way in the US. However, most don't realize that the United States is still one of the biggest producers and consumers of child pornography in the world[14]. We're not talking about consenting adults, or even about the exploitation of women, but about *children* used in sexually abu-sive material for adult pleasure.

It's a global problem, and it's one that affects millions of families in the United States. These are the facts I deal with on a daily basis, and they don't lie. It's not pretty. There is no sugarcoating what little boys and girls go through because of sick, perverted adults.

After this, many women do not like to talk to me anymore. I'm very sorry to pull people out of their comfort zone; but I must speak for the voiceless. Our rescued children are often found behind closed doors, in tiny, filthy shacks, or hiding on dark streets. Their voices are not heard. Their suffering is in secret. And it's only getting worse. During the COVID-19 pandemic, people became less interested in human trafficking, which allowed groups involved in human trafficking to reorganize and flourish[15], especially with online activity, trapping young girls through deception and grooming.[16]

Following my car accident, it took a long time - years - for me to feel I could speak loudly, or laugh out loud. My amnesia and ongoing physical challenges made me quiet, submissive and underconfident in many areas of my life. But this calling God placed on my life, to rescue, restore, and raise vulnerable, abused children, also restored to me something I'd lost for many years - my voice. It's what so many children do not have; something they've been prohibited from using, for fear that worse things will come on them, or on a younger sibling. I've become their voice as well, helping them to leave their situations, speaking out against their aggressors, telling their stories that otherwise would never be told.

Allow me to share some of them with you here.

* * *

CALEB

I was working on a case when I got a knock at my office door. There stood Caleb - dirty and silent. He'd been living on the streets. No one to love him or care for him. Few people on Earth have suffered as Caleb had during his 12 years before becoming our Village son. Caleb was abandoned, abused, exploited and trafficked. The traumas of his childhood left him with a severe speech impediment and cognitive disabilities.

A few days after his arrival, Caleb joined us for prayer and Bible reading for the first time. We were all together with the other kids, in the large meeting area of VCH. I asked Caleb if he believed there was a God who loved him. He looked around him, then looked at me and answered quietly, "No."

The rest of the kids smiled and shook their heads, knowing that God was real, and that Mamá Nicole would not leave it there. I didn't, of course. I said to him, "I hope we can convince you otherwise, because there is a God, and He loves you very much!" Then we continued with our time of singing, Bible reading and prayer together - followed by some delicious warm chocolate milk from the state of Oaxaca.

A few weeks later, I was chatting with some of my smaller boys and told them that we'd be celebrating December birthdays the next day. They asked me what we'd be eating, and I said it'd be *tamales* - a traditional, delicious Mexican dish made from corn and other ingredients.

"What kind of tamales?" the boys asked me.

Being a jokester, I replied, "Mouse tamales."

Most of them giggled and said, "No way, Mamá! Gross! You know we can't eat rodents!"

But little Caleb did not even blink. He replied, "Mice are not bad, especially if you have peppers and lime to squeeze on them."

We all stopped laughing. "Are you playing with us, or have you really eaten mice before, Caleb?" I asked him.

"Yes, I have," he answered. "When I was really hungry and that was all I could catch."

Caleb stayed with us until he turned 18 - his smile lighting up the room, his hugs strong. Two years after his arrival, he raised his hand during devotions, ready to share his testimony with the other children. Although his extreme childhood abuse severely impaired his abilities to learn at school, his spiritual progress flourished. Upon leaving the Village home, he went to live with a pastor and his family. Praise God, Caleb got baptized and has continued to preach and share his testimony with others. He is studying photography, and we recently gave him his first camera. He has a voice, because God gave him one through us.

* * *

HADASSAH

She was so little when I saw her walking to me from a distance. She was with the young men I'd sent out to look for her once again, just as we'd been doing every Saturday for ten months. But this time they found her!

Can it really be? Did they finally find her? I thought. Yes, they had! Hadassah was frightened and dirty ... and had been so very abused.

She tensed up and hung her head low when I embraced her. Her hair was matted and filthy. I was unable to get her clothes off to bathe her, for they were many sizes too small. I had to use a pair of kitchen scissors to cut off her crusty pants. I looked for the barely readable tag to check the size - it was a size 4. It was important to know the clothes size so that when we found her birth certificate and discovered her age, I could calculate her case a little better.

A year later, after much paperwork and investigation, we retrieved Hadassah's birth certificate. We discovered that she was eight years old when she was rescued. Her Mom had died when she was barely four. I realized with shock that *Hadassah had worn the same clothes for four years.*

After their Mom's death, Hadassah and her sister Hope had

been left with their abusive father, who allowed horrendous, perverted atrocities to be performed on them both over and over again. We were able to find both sisters within just four months, and they became our precious daughters, along with their older brother - and a few years later, their younger brother, who had also been trapped in exploitation. They all grew up at VCH and were a true joy (and a bit of work!) to raise.

A year after Hadassah and Hope's arrival, the state authorities called me to take the siblings to the hospital. Their father was dying. He wanted to see them. We did not know what to expect, and approached his bed with caution. To our surprise, he broke down, repenting of all that he had done to them, and asking their forgiveness as we stood at his bedside. Their father gave his life to Jesus ... and then passed away.

* * *

GINA

Gina had just turned 12 when she was rescued from downtown Mexico City. Her own mother had been sold as a baby to a family who harmed and used her body her entire life. Gina was conceived as a result of rape, and from birth she too was considered nothing more than an object, a means of making money for others. It's yet another tragic story of a little girl who has lived through the gravest of abominations.

The poor child did not know her vowels or how to count to ten when she arrived at VCH. But when she started to go to school she discovered a new world of knowledge and wonder. She devoured books - even though she still struggled to read. But the desire was there. Gina is now able to do what a lot of children take for granted.

* * *

FLOR

It took five months of trying to rescue her. Little Flor had seen me trying many times - but each time I was threatened and had to back off. I knew of her case, and I would not stop. Flor was being beaten, and raped, and tortured. She would be left in a barrel full of cold water - up to her neck - with her hands tied behind her back, so she had to fight to stay above water all night long. These are tactics used by perpetrators in order to secure total submission.

Finally our attempts to rescue her succeeded, and so began Flor's list of "firsts". The first time she slept in a bed. Her first pizza for lunch. Her first time playing freely on the swings. She came and hugged me at least 20 times randomly throughout the day, thanking me for rescuing her and telling me how much she loved me. She was a brilliant little girl. She remembered seeing me all those times. Thankfully, no longer would she be tortured and abused. Now she was free.

There are few true miracle stories ... but this was definitely one of them. In less than 3 weeks after Flor's rescue, I was able to give her permanently to an amazing family - her distant family. It was a fairy-tale come true. I'd been in another district all day, pressing charges, giving hours of statements and declarations, taking a child for a medical exam with the justice court's doctor, and making more appointments for the next week. It was exhausting.

But to be able to end the day coming back and giving little Flor to a wonderful forever family, who received her with open arms and warm love, was priceless. Sweet little Flor kissed me goodbye and said to me, "I will love you forever." It made my heart swell. It makes it all so very worth it.

* * *

Twice a year we make a trip with all the children to the beach. These trips inevitably include at least one vehicle getting stuck in the sand and one child throwing up. But what outings they are! For most, it's the first time they've ever been to the beach - the first time they've seen the majestic ocean, felt the sand in their toes, walked along the shore and sensed the sand give way as the water moves out, heard the lapping of the waves and the calls of the seagulls, and looked out to the horizon and wondered what was out there beyond.

At the beach we teach the children about forgiveness, and letting go. Forgiving does not mean saying or believing that what the perpetrators did was right. Neither does it mean we refrain from seeking justice or pressing charges, allowing the bad guys to go free. It doesn't even mean we shouldn't pray daily for Jesus to return to judge and bring God's vengeance on unrepentant evildoers.

On the contrary! Forgiveness, first and foremost, is an act of obedience to the God who rescued them. It frees the children from anger, resentment, and the constant remembrance and reliving of what the wicked people did to them. It means the children can move on; that they can begin to learn how to be children of the Most High, understanding the forgiveness God offers each one of us through the sacrifice of Jesus Christ, and offering that forgiveness in their hearts to their perpetrators.

It is so important for abused children to take this step of faith in forgiving. It is necessarily a step of faith because they are trusting in the Lord to work in them in an unseen way through the cleansing blood of Jesus. It takes them one step closer to total healing. Amy Carmichael once said, "If I say, 'Yes, I forgive, but I cannot forget,' as though the God, who twice a day washes all the sands on all the shores of all the world, could not wash such memories from my mind, then I know nothing of Calvary love."

As the children stand in a line at the shore's edge, tightly holding a seashell in their hand, they listen for the count of three and throw their shell into the ocean, signifying their letting go of the anger and bitterness they've harbored in their hearts. It's one of the most poignant actions the children undertake.

* * *

I don't tell you all this for a pat on the back, but to give God all the glory. I don't do it alone - it takes a strong team. Anonymous phone calls, help from state authorities, countless late nights and searching, and courageous neighbors who help us. It really does take a Village.

A visitor once said to me, as she loved on the babies and toddlers and helped me care for them each day, "I don't understand. I just look at these precious children and wonder - how can their parents not want them?"

That is a good question. It's a question I still cannot really answer.

Drugs, alcohol and other addictions are a major cause, but mainly it's because they have never been given the true gospel, and because loving, godly church communities in Mexico are practically non-existent.

There. I said it. Gonna keep fighting. And finding Jesus-followers who are ready to join me. We are on the Lord's side. He has the victory. Every child's life counts.

CHAPTER EIGHTEEN

The Training Ground

So then, be careful how you walk, not as unwise people but as wise, making the most of your time, because the days are evil. - Ephesians 5:15-16 (NASB)

Every wise workman takes his tools away from the work from time to time that they may be ground and sharpened; so does the only-wise Jehovah take his ministers oftentimes away into darkness and loneliness and trouble, that he may sharpen and prepare them for harder work in his service. – Robert Murray McCheyne

A FEW YEARS back Jason and I were invited to the home of a young Christian couple, Ricardo and Margot. They were interested in our work at VCH, and we'd been getting to know them, enjoying their company. We sat down with them at their kitchen table. They had many questions; during the evening they fired them off, one after the other.

"Did you have any formal training for what you've under-taken, Nicole?" Ricardo asked.

"Well, over the years I've had to wing it a lot," I admitted. "I never did get my nursing degree, but I gotta say, caring for so many children, I've had to learn a lot on the go. I am constant-ly giving shots and administering IVs. On any given day I might be giving medication for pain from a wisdom tooth extraction, or a sprained wrist, or to slow contractions before we make it to hospital. But God is so gracious! He truly has given me what I need to help the children."

"In what ways?" Ricardo asked again.

"It's as if my whole life has been a training ground for what God was preparing me to do, to rescue children. I've come to see how much He has equipped me through my experiences. Be-ing a missionary kid in Guatemala and Peru, it all started there; but let me tell you about what I've learned as a result of the ac-cident I had."

"Go on," said Margot, smiling, as she poured us some tea.

"I think about my wreck, way back in 1993. So many lessons came out of that. The accident caused my brain to shut down. I couldn't work out what was real and what was not. I couldn't re-member my past, and I didn't know who I was. I was *totally* de-pendent on others to bring me back to a world that made sense. It took a lot of time and patience on their part to help me heal and regain what I'd lost. They kept repeating truths over and over to me, until I was able to understand and accept them."

"I see," said Margot, nodding. She was a psychologist, an expert in caring for children who had experienced trauma, and she began to consider what I was saying. "The children you care for now - they all have different backgrounds, but what they have in common is how defenseless they are. They have to de-pend on others to help them make sense of a world that, at least for them, has turned against them."

"Exactly!" I replied. "They're like young plants, pulled up and left exposed to the elements. They need others to rescue and restore them until they can put down roots that will give them strength and stability."

"That's what James says in the Bible," said Jason. "'Religion that God our Father accepts as pure and faultless is this: to look after orphans and widows in their distress and to keep oneself from being polluted by the world.' That's what Nicole has been doing - looking after orphans and widows, the most vulnerable in this world."

I nodded, and said, "I love that verse." Then I continued. "I also think a lot about my therapies at the hospital in Corpus Christi. They taught me so many life lessons. I had a strict routine: I was bathed at this time, was fed at that time, received visitors at other times ... I remember I felt like a prisoner, but looking back I can see how that structure and order gave me a framework in which I felt safe and secure; I didn't have to wonder what was going to happen next. And that helped my mind to focus on getting better."

I paused for a moment, and went on: "I was once taught this phrase, and it's been close to me ever since: *Law is for order, and boundaries are for your protection.* And the children I raise - they don't have to worry any more about what's going to happen or when they're going to eat their next meal, because that's all worked out for them daily. So keeping a routine and having boundaries helps their levels of anxiety to go down."

"What other things did God teach you, Nicole?" Ricardo asked.

I thought again. "You know, lots of people spoke discouraging words to me while I was in the hospital: that I'd never recover, never remember, never walk again, never live a 'normal' life.

"So when I'd listen to the children's stories about their lives before they'd been rescued, underneath all the horror of the abuse, the neglect, and the torture were beliefs they carried about themselves and their world. Words they'd heard shouted, which they'd silently repeat to themselves as they lay in bed or sat alone. *You're worthless. I can't stand to look at you. Nobody loves you. I never wanted you. I wish you were dead. You were an accident. You messed up my life. God hates you. You'll never amount to anything. It's all your fault. Don't tell me what you want, I don't care. I don't want you here.*"

I stopped to take some tea. My mouth had grown dry just from saying these words out loud. Then I went on.

"Now people had not said those things to me, but from my experience in the hospital I knew the power of words and how they could change a person's outlook on life and the future. Other people spoke words of encouragement to me. Those words were like little precious jewels that I could hold onto, like that beautiful bracelet Saul gave me - remember, Jason?"

He nodded, probably remembering how I gave it away.

"Those words gave me hope and life, and helped me lift up my thoughts to what I could do and become. They helped me remember that I served a great and loving Father God who worked miracles, who had promised me He'd be with me always.

"I knew that being a child of God gave me an identity that no-one could take away, and that He and He only was in control of my future, not any human being, no matter how powerful or evil they might be. I remembered my dear parents, and Jason, and my brothers, who spoke to me each day and reminded me of who I was when I awoke and couldn't remember anything.

"And so, in the same way, I began to speak words of life to these precious children - words that would change their beliefs about their identity and their self-worth."

"What sort of words do you tell the children?" Margot asked, leaning forward.

I took a deep breath. *"You are loved. You are valued. You are safe. You will never be hurt here. We're your new family. Nothing that happened is your fault. You are innocent. God loves you, and He brought you to us. You are not a burden. You are a blessing. You are not the problem. You are the answer. The future is yours. Your healing has begun. We love you, and are so happy that you are now part of our Village family."*

I paused. "And this one: *You are not alone.*"

Margot wiped a tear from her eye with her knuckle.

I went on. "You know, people also tried to force me to remember things, and recover at the speed *they* wanted, not at what *I* could do. I was accused of faking my lack of improvement, of not trying hard enough. People assumed I could do things, when I still couldn't. Does that sound familiar to you, Margot?"

"Of course," she answered. "Each child is different, and processes things differently. Some heal quickly; some take a long time to let go of hurtful memories. Some simply can't learn, because the trauma they experienced has blocked areas of their brain from functioning properly. Each child has to go at their own pace, and we need to be mindful and patient as we help them in their process of restoration. Sometimes it takes a lot of repetition."

We sipped our tea. "Nicole, what about the importance of Scripture?" Jason reminded me.

"Yes, God taught me a lot there. My father would read to me from the Bible every single day that he was with me in the hospital. It helped my mind and my spirit recall things that were familiar to me from my past. And at the children's home, they are constantly surrounded by Scripture so that they'll discover the true and living God, their Heavenly Father. We do a lot of memorization of Scripture. Every day. The children spur each other on to learn and to remember."

"What has God taught you about prayer?" asked Ricardo.

"Prayer has been an absolute constant. So many people prayed for me while I was in the hospital. I know that my healing is an answer to prayer.

"When I was in Xochiatipan I would write our newsletters, asking people to pray daily for the both of us, and for our family. And now we ask for prayer for every rescued child in our care - and God has answered those prayers, more times than we can possibly count. And I teach the children to pray to their Heavenly Father - He's a Father who listens, cares, provides, and heals."

I stopped and looked at Margot and Ricardo. They were holding hands and their eyes were shining.

"I think this is the ministry we've been praying for," said Margot. "We have the same heart as you to help the children."

Since this conversation and many more besides, we have been beyond blessed to have Margot and Ricardo (and more recently, their little baby boy Benji) walk alongside us in this journey, bringing their wisdom, love and professional help and care to our family and the children's home.

* * *

Rescues, restoration and raising children don't just happen on their own. There is so much work involved: investigative work, negotiating, acts of bravery, discipline, care, listening and love. Over time, the Lord has provided a team of like-minded people who helped me take on the load. I've received constant support from our mission organization and donors - people who believe in what we do and support us.

But above all, it takes faith in God and His promises. Because our Lord Jesus has told us that if we ask anything in His name, He will do it[14] - and we know that God's heart is with the

---

14. John 16:23

orphan, the widow, the foreigner and the destitute.[17] Did God say these words? Are His words real? True? Should we take heed and obey them?

CHAPTER NINETEEN

Landslide!

We are afflicted in every way, but not crushed; perplexed, but not despairing; persecuted, but not abandoned; struck down, but not destroyed; always carrying around in the body the dying of Jesus, so that the life of Jesus may also be revealed in our body. - 2 Corinthians 4:8-10 (NASB)

Life is pitiful, death so familiar, suffering and pain so common, yet I would not be anywhere else. Do not wish me out of this or in any way seek to get me out, for I will not be got out while this trial is on. These are my people, God has given them to me, and I will live or die for Him and His glory. - Gladys Aylward

HAVE YOU EVER heard of Gladys Aylward? This tiny un-married British missionary traveled across the entire country of Russia by train and mule in 1931, to China, to help a fellow Christian woman share the gospel at an inn for mule drivers - and ended up becoming an official inspector of wom-en's feet, helping them to undo (literally) centuries of tradition of foot binding, while also preaching the gospel and liberating their souls.

Gladys never had children of her own, but she cared for many abandoned children whom she rescued. During the Japanese invasion of 1938, Gladys led a group of more than 100 orphaned children - between 3 and 16 years of age - away from the danger of the Japanese armies; although she was wounded and ill and collapsed upon arrival, they crossed "impassable" mountains by God's grace and made it to safety.

It sounds like something out of a movie, doesn't it? Most of us would probably say that Gladys' life was totally unlike our own.

But I can relate in part. It wasn't the Japanese who attacked us, but the whiplash from a hurricane called Earl, August 6, 2016.

Earl swept across the Atlantic from the western coast of Africa, hitting Belize first as a tropical storm. As a hurricane, it wasn't the biggest ever, but it moved north into Mexico and significantly struck the states of Veracruz and Puebla with an entire month's rainfall in 24 hours. Thousands of homes were lost, and over 100 people died; in nearby Huauchinango alone there were at least 13 deaths.[18] What caused the damage? Landslides.

I've been in earthquakes before in Peru and Mexico, and the Village had even gone through a landslide back in 2010, but this was much worse. Living on the side of a mountain, we'd terraced and tried to stabilize the area as much as we could. The day of the hurricane, we'd just finished painting the school rooms and pavilion. It was wonderful, after so many years of construction, to finally say joyfully "We're done!" And it looked amazing. The kids were ecstatic. Papá Jasón was away, preaching in Mexico City. Some national missionaries had just returned from a 5-day evangelistic trip high up in the mountains - exhausted but blessed, enjoying being back with their wives and walking around in shorts and flip flops after having hiked so much the previous days.

Then came the nightmare.

On August 5th, the wind howled and the rain kept pounding until everything around us was just water and mud and noise. Water was flowing down from the hill above us; streams of water ran off the roofs, and the river below had swelled up and flooded.

The next afternoon I had a gut feeling something was going to happen. I could feel rumbling in the ground below me. I called our workers together, telling them to gather all the children out of the pavilion and to keep them in the upstairs schoolroom, only coming down for meals. "Angel," I spoke to one of the missionary workers, "I feel like we need to be prepared."

Angel looked at me and raised his finger as if teaching me a lesson. "You've gotta have faith in God, Sister Nicole," he said to me stoically. (Mexican Christians often refer to each other as *Brother* and *Sister*.)

I shook my head. "I don't know ... I don't know how to describe it, Angel, but I feel like the whole mountain's going to come down on us." The rumbling continued under my feet.

Angel insisted I was being pessimistic.

As we were talking, standing on the edge of the hill overlooking the river and valley below, we heard a noise. Suddenly, water began to shoot out of the side of the mountain - like a fireman's hose on full pressure. "Do you see that?" I exclaimed to Angel over the noise, pointing vigorously at the water bursting forth. "Now where's that water coming from?"

As I was speaking, all at once and directly in front of us, our macadamia, avocado and peach trees simply uprooted themselves and flipped over, splashing mud on us and leaving us standing on a precarious ledge of concrete overhanging the exposed red dirt below. "Do you believe me now?" I shouted above the noise as we began to run. Angel was shocked, but believed.

We sprang into action. I'd already prepared the important documents and papers that we'd need to take with us, and we got the children ready to leave. Unfortunately, we didn't have a lot of vehicles - they'd been lent out to others a few days earlier. We only had a van and two trucks, and night was approaching. The police drove up to tell us we had to evacuate - but we were already on it.

There were more than just children to evacuate. We also had unwed mothers with babies with us, a pregnant teenager, and some elderly people, including a man with only one leg and men and women with dementia and Alzheimer's whom we'd found on the streets.

It was just me, Angel and a few helpers, with about 60 people to organize, including my teenage niece and nephew who happened to be visiting. Two young men, sons I'd raised named Manuel and Javier, stayed at the Village. They refused to leave, arguing that someone needed to be there to stop others from coming later and looting the place. We couldn't convince them otherwise.

We piled everyone else into the three vehicles, grabbing children with both hands and elderly people who were trying to wander off. Once everyone was in, squeezed together, we slammed the doors and I said, "Go." As the three vehicles drove down the driveway to the road below, we could see the entire mountain behind us slowly but inexorably collapse over each of our buildings, dragging everything down. I felt totally gutted ... but so glad to have made it out, and it was no time to stand still and grieve.

We drove as far as we could in our vehicles, as quickly as we could under the stormy, volatile conditions, until it was impossible to go further - which was only to Xaltepuxtla, the next town along, less than 3 miles (3.8 km) away. Telephone poles and trees had fallen across the road; it was too treacherous.

We abandoned our vehicles and organized ourselves. My assistant, Martha, took the mothers, the babies, and the elderly people to a house on the other side of Xaltepuxtla which belonged to her aunt. Many of the people had to be carried there, through waist-high mud. People from the town helped them get there safely. Thank God, Martha's aunt's house had a concrete foundation and was not affected by the landslide. All those vulnerable people made it to safety.

Meanwhile, the rest of us had to walk to the next town over - Las Colonias, less than two miles away. Under normal circumstances we could have easily walked there in less than an hour; but in the middle of the storm it took us about 6 hours to get there. The night was pitch black and still raining heavily, with only the lightning flashes illuminating everyone's anxious faces.

There were about 50 children with us. We adults were carrying a baby or small child on each hip, picking our way carefully through the thick, slippery mud filled with branches and who knew what else, avoiding crashing trees and falling poles and cables, climbing over cars that were stranded in the mud, not knowing if any people were even inside the cars. Each movement was slow and difficult, and the journey seemed to last forever.

Moving so slowly along through the wind and rain, shivering with cold and fright, trying not to slip or get sucked into the deep mud, a feeling of doom began to come over many of the children. My nephew would ask me questions that betrayed his fear: "Aunt Nicole? Are we going to die? Am I in a nightmare? Is this a disaster movie?"

Other children would scream out, "¡Voy a morir! I'm going to die! Mamá Nicole, will I go to heaven or to hell?" It was a mammoth task. It was all I could do to keep going and try to motivate everyone to keep moving.

It was 2 am when we finally reached Las Colonias, soaking wet, filthy, and utterly exhausted. We reached the place of a dear friend named Arturo, and from there he loaded us all up in his vehicles and drove us to Xicotepec, where we had a college home for older kids. It was cramped, and we arrived with nothing - the little we'd taken in the vehicles we'd left inside them - but we were safe, and we were able to stay there while everything was getting sorted out. We had no idea how much of the Village was lost.

We were so thankful to God that we all made it out safely without injury, given the circumstances and the number of injuries and deaths from landslides in the area. We were also grateful for our beloved friends and helpers from Xicotepec, Dr. Morales and Margarita, who made a huge house available to us, with a large, open courtyard. They allowed us to rent it at a good price for as long as we needed. Kind people provided money for a playground to be installed in the courtyard for the children.

Yet, we could not help but mourn our beloved Village and feel an enormous sense of despair as we returned to look over the damage. So much hard work over the years, to have it be destroyed. One of the pavilion's pylons had been bent from the inexorable weight of the mud. Pathways past the dorms had collapsed down the hill. There was just so much dirt and mud that had pushed its way into and over the Village.

This was the second landslide in 6 years. Was God trying to tell us something? Was He unhappy with what we were doing? Was this a sign from God or an attack of the enemy? We sought His guidance through much prayer and fasting. We could see areas that we needed to work at to improve, especially regarding people who had been a part of our ministry, but who had in different ways betrayed our trust and worked against the ministry. We repented, and asked God to direct us. And He gave us peace - peace that this was not punishment from Him, and that we would start again.

At the beginning I'd felt there was no way we could go back to La Gallera or repair the place. We began to look at buying other properties - but good land was out of our budget, and it was such a difficult, discouraging thing to have to start all over again. We prayed and discussed it a lot, and finally decided we needed to return, in the same way that most people in the area had decided to do. It turned out that the pavilion, cafeteria, and a few dorms were taken out by the landslide, but other parts were still intact.

We set to work. There was so much to do. The mud had settled at chest-level and had to be removed slowly. We had to create new terracing on the side of the mountain, plant more trees, and build rock walls along the edges. New concrete dorms would replace the wooden cabins, and the big pavilion had to be rebuilt. Safe areas for any future disasters needed to be created. But we received a massive amount of support from our friends, family, and supporters, who generously donated to make it happen.

We began to grow excited again. We could reinvent our old place. New bathrooms with sewage and drainage replaced the outhouses of the past; now we'd have *flushable toilets!* It took 2 ½ years of living away in Xicotepec, but in January 2019 we finally moved back to our Village premises which the children had loved and missed. The move took four days. There was great celebration.

Once again, we'd been uprooted - literally! But we were not undone. Afflicted, but not crushed. God was still with us - He replanted us and allowed us to flourish again.

CHAPTER TWENTY

The Toll

But you be watchful in all things, endure afflictions, do the work of an evangelist, fulfill your ministry. For I am already being poured out as a drink offering, and the time of my departure is at hand.- 2 Timothy 4:5-6 (NKJV)

Christ has paid the full price for our redemption, but our walk with God on a daily basis will cost us much. Are we willing, cheerfully, to pay the cost? – AW Tozer

CRYSTAL METH IS a demon. It is killing our youth and causing consumers' babies and children to suffer grave atrocities.[19]

It was a rare case. The 22-year-old mother, herself a victim of heinous crimes and abuse since childhood, came crying, begging for a chance in life for herself and her children. She asked us to help her be detoxed. It was not easy - Jason had begun a ministry to help men and youths struggling from drug and alcohol addiction; but it was only for males, so we had to pay for a place out-of-state for this young mother.

Meanwhile, her three children arrived at VCH with absolutely nothing but urgent medical needs. Our pets lived better than they had. At VCH the baby, Tori, had her first bottle of milk ever. Her mother had nursed her; this meant that the baby was also a crystal meth addict.

The nights were long as Tori detoxed. Every night she would lie in my arms while I sang, prayed, rocked, and wept for hours. She writhed in pain and sweated. And she would not - could not - sleep; instead she lay there twitching, crying, raging, threshing.

It took a long time for me to figure out how she slept best - laying on top of me. She nestled her head against my heart and, in doing so, finally slept for hours. I wondered to myself: *Can she hear my heart beating and telling her how much she is loved?* She played with my hair. She even smiled in her sleep. She'd begun to heal.

But each night I hated drugs more. And more. *Crystal meth, I hate you.*

* * *

I have to admit, it hasn't been easy. In fact, I'm the first to recognize that. And why should it be different? God Himself promised me it would be a long and hard road.

Physically, there have been many battles. Over the years I've struggled with numerous health repercussions due to my car accident, and this has brought me to have myriads of tests and diagnoses, leading to multiple surgeries - 34, in fact, but who's counting? Every six months or so my stomach shuts down, refusing to digest anything, and my intestines become paralyzed. The vertebrae in my back have disintegrated and sometimes also cause paralysis and much pain. In fact, I'm often in pain.

There are many times when I lie on my couch and just try to muster up strength for the next task. There are moments when I'm so looking forward to ticking off the final item on my list of

Things to Do Today - have a shower and go to bed - and then the phone rings or visitors turn up unexpectedly. And in Mexico, what must we do? Be hospitable! Sit with them and offer coffee or hot chocolate and some sweet bread left over from the night's supper.

Sometimes I'm so tired, sore, and overwhelmed from the rescues, I feel like Elijah after his great victory over the prophets of Baal, only to be threatened by Queen Jezebel and end up hiding in a small place[15]; and I pray to God, "God, just let me die and disappear. I cannot do this anymore."

But these moments don't last. God always picks me up and shows me how I am loved, valued, and needed. When I'm feeling exhausted my teenage girls lend me their arms for support as I walk down to the pavilion and back, and they massage me at night. When I've been away from the Village, I come back and am embraced and kissed by 50 people, receiving over 50 handwritten letters and drawings.

Over the years, people have asked me many questions. One of the most common is how I find the strength to keep going. All I can say in reply is - "GOD." Period. He is my sustainer and source of all strength. The Lord always provides people who come alongside me and strengthen me - including those who live far away and stand in the gap for me in prayer.

Some concerned people tell me, "You mustn't take on more than you can handle." That *sounds* great ... but what do I do with a little girl whose father just died, leaving her mother defenseless and living in abject poverty, and Child Protection Authorities asking me to take her in? I cannot NOT take her. So I trust God to help me handle it - because He is the one who has called me to do this.

I trust Him to help me make one more rescue.

The battles haven't just been physical. I went through a long

---

15. 1 Kings 19:1-4

period of emotional toil. For a number of years and before I had professional psychologists working alongside me, I struggled with thoughts of anger and resentment. At night, exhausted and wishing to sleep, my mind would mull over the stories I'd hear of men, young and old, using little children and teenagers to fulfill their sick sexual appetites. I'd hear the children speak, sobbing, of the sexual violence imposed on them and the threats of harming smaller siblings if they told anyone or did not comply, and I grew increasingly upset and bitter.

Gradually, my heart began to harden against men in general. Who did they think they were, using their brute strength and positions of authority to take advantage of little girls and boys? Just how many men were pedophiles and porn addicts? How many men were loving husbands outwardly, while harboring secrets of unspeakable acts behind their wives' backs?

I went through a very difficult period when I felt I couldn't trust a single man - not even my own husband. Having heard so many horrific stories of trauma inflicted at the hands of men and seen the cool indifference of men in authority who lifted no finger to help, I became cynical, suspecting every man I knew of unfaithfulness and sexual depravity.

It hurt my relationship with Jason for a time, including our own intimacy, even though he was always faithful and never gave me reason to suspect him of any untoward behavior. Even so, my words became harsh, accusatory, and judgmental towards men, all the time thinking to myself, "They all deserve it - they're all rotten. You can't trust a man."

It took time for me to realize that it wasn't only the children who needed counseling. I was suffering from depression, as well as an emotional duress known as secondhand or vicarious trauma. This is commonly experienced by those who work in law enforcement, emergency medical services, and war zones.[20] Those who work with victims of trauma are affected when they witness the events or hear their stories of the traumatic incidents. Secondhand trauma is directly related to the higher rates of suicide among law enforcement officers and war veterans in particular.

In my own case, it manifested through my negative emotional reactions to everything and everyone, difficulty sleeping, and health issues. My mind continued to dwell on what had happened to these children, and my anger and mistrust against men continued to grow. And it was no fault of my husband.

In 2018, I went through one of the very lowest points in my life. I was living, for the greater part of my time, while my daughter finished high school and prepared for college, in the state of Missouri, traveling to VCH in Mexico for 1-2 weeks at a time. Jason was mostly involved in other projects in Mexico; he'd established the drug and alcohol rehabilitation centers for young men and boys. He had so much going on. The rehab centers took up a lot of his time and effort. On top of this, he continued to visit the churches he'd planted, encourage the national missionaries, and motivate Christians to start new businesses with a Christian ethos.

Instead of feeling relaxed and refreshed during the time I spent away from Mexico, I felt as if I was drowning. There were constant phone calls from the children's home, describing their usual stresses; new cases of trafficking that authorities would call me about daily; we were going through family issues; and I had even more health challenges (such as getting typhoid fever on a recurring basis). I also found myself with extra time each evening to think and reflect on things that had happened in the past. All of this combined to make me feel exhausted, inadequate and overwhelmed, caught in situations I didn't know how to get out of.

I began to feel helpless and weak, that I wasn't doing enough, that I was a stumbling block to others' progress. I became convinced that I was everybody's problem, and that they'd all be better off without me. This was a lie - a lie from the devil, but I swallowed it, hook, line, and sinker.

What made things even worse was that I felt I had no one I could talk to. We'd grown up being taught that missionaries were strong and reliant only on the Lord, and that counseling or psychological care was unnecessary, even secular or worldly. I also felt many times that even though I wanted to share with people some of what the children had told me, to get it off my chest and deal with it verbally, that it would only traumatize my listeners - many people I'd shared even a small amount of information with couldn't handle hearing about children being abused, abandoned or trafficked, and they would ask me to stop talking.

For several years we'd been working with a new mission organization which supported many ministries like ours. However, they also made it clear to us that they were ministers, not marriage counselors or therapists. Their responses to me were short and unsympathetic. And so I did not receive the type of care I needed from them either. I'd pray on my own, read the Bible, sing and listen to worship music, but the ugly feelings remained and the memories continued to surface.

It was Sunday evening, September 9, 2018. I was in Missouri with my daughter, Jasmine, 17 at the time. I can't say exactly what was going on in my head. But I began to embark on a set of deliberate steps.

I spent the day cleaning the house, making sure it was spotless. I cleaned and vacuumed the car and made sure all the bills were paid. After this I went through my social media accounts - and deleted them all. I entered Jasmine's room where she was sleeping, kissed her forehead goodnight and prayed for her, then went to the kitchen with a container of strong sleeping pills I'd been given in one of my typhoid episodes. I counted out a certain number of them and placed them on the counter. I turned on the faucet and used my hand to drink the water so I wouldn't dirty another glass and have to wash it. One by one I swallowed the pills. Then I went to my bedroom, got into bed, and closed my eyes.

* * *

It took a long time for my daughter to realize something was wrong. The next morning Jason called her and asked her to check on me, because I wasn't answering my phone. Jasmine was just glad to see me finally sleeping so well. But Jason began to insist that she try to wake me up - he knew that I *never* slept past 7:30 am, no matter how tired I was; and it was well past that hour. He was growing more and more concerned.

* * *

I thank God people came to my rescue. I am glad I did not die that day. I woke up in the hospital four days later. I received psychiatric care. Even when I was faithless, God remained faithful.[16] And He continued to hold me in His hand, even though I was at rock bottom, again.

* * *

After this incredibly difficult time, the Lord provided me with people who reassured me of my own worth as His child and reminded me of my identity in Him and not in my own works. Later, He brought just the right people into my path - such as Margot and other counselors - who have helped me beyond comprehension to deal with these issues and heal those parts of my mind and soul that were hurting and confused. They have provided me with the ongoing care and counseling that I con-

---

16. 2 Timothy 2:13

tinue to need. And they love me enough to tell me when and where I go wrong.

Part of my healing was realizing that this was not an issue about men, but about human nature in general. Men and women - we are all fallen creatures before our Lord. I had to realize that there are good, upright, godly men, and there are dangerous, perverse, evil women, as well as the reverse.

It turns out that many sex traffickers - the pimps, the ones who befriend and recruit the young girls, or the ones who keep a lookout for police operatives - are women.[21] In some countries in the world, as much as 60% of sex traffickers are women.[22] A lot of these women have at some point been sexually exploited themselves. Rather than making them more empathetic to the plight of young girls, it can desensitize and harden them.

Again, it's not just men who abuse and abandon their children. I've had hundreds of cases where the abuser was the mother, the grandmother, or the stepmother of the child. One mother, when confronted by government agents coming to take away her four abused, malnourished children, shouted at them, "Take them away! And don't bring them back - if you do, I'll throw them down the well!" And many others, both men and women, are accomplices to abusive actions, remaining silent or taking the side of the aggressor and accusing the child of breaking up the family.

In this way, I was able to take a step back from my own ideas about men, and understand the problems we were facing as those of sin and evil that permeate the hearts of all people, to a greater or lesser degree. It brought me to repent of my own sin and gave me a renewed sense of God's grace in my own life.

There have been times, many times, when I have prayed with tears and asked, "Lord God, why do these horrible things happen to the innocent? Why do they have to suffer?" I can't give an easy answer to this. What I do know is that God sees the big picture which we cannot in this life. And He is coming again to judge the sins of every human being - every person who of their own free will has deliberately chosen to do evil and go against God and not repent.

In continuing the spiritual disciplines my parents taught me, I've grown closer to my Father God and love Him more, knowing that all things will make sense in the end. And I pray fervently, like the beloved Apostle John, "*Come, Lord Jesus.*"[17]

Still, every single day I get mad; truly, it's impossible not to. My adrenaline rises with every rescue, and I grow angry every time I have to hear the victims tell their stories again. Many times I cuss under my breath as I hold a child detoxing from drugs, tend to the children's wounds, and treat their sexually transmitted diseases - knowing they're not curable, only controllable. Those feelings of secondhand trauma still often lurk close by.

* * *

Many people also ask me, "What is the hardest part of raising so many children?" Jason and I would sometimes talk about this and think deeply about our answer.

The hardest part of raising these children? Letting them go.

Do not get me wrong - I am all about adoption and foster care. But it is still hard: the unknown, the fear, the what if's. What will their futures hold? Will they truly be alright? There is so much pressure ... and my mind does not stop dwelling on these questions and doubts.

Each time we let them go it reminds me that we were only a stepping stone in the lives of many. Given, hundreds of children remember us, call us, visit us, and so on. But for most of the babies and little ones who are restored to a safe family member, placed in a caring foster home, or adopted into a loving fami-

---

17. Revelation 22:20, NASB

ly, we are only a crossroads for them. A safe place. A holding ground. A healing spot. They will never know the agony and determination it cost to win their rescue and freedom. They will never remember the endless sleepless nights I spent bringing them back to health and healing. They will probably never even know my name or that I ever existed.

But we will always remember them.

* * *

Yes, living as a missionary in Mexico and rescuing children from hellish lives has taken a toll on my own life. I can't deny this. I'm not going to sugarcoat it with, "But really, I'm living my best life", or shout out, "I am blessed and highly favored!", and I certainly can't say that I enjoy incredible yearly vacations to the Bahamas. I gave all that up when I surrendered my life to Jesus.

It's what He tells all of His disciples: "If anyone wants to come after Me, he must deny himself, take up his cross daily, and follow Me."[18] The German theologian Dietrich Bonhoeffer wrote this about being a Christian: "When Christ calls a man, he bids him come and die."[23] How can we think that picking up and carrying our cross is going to be easy? Are we looking for a soft padded cross to carry? There is no such thing.

Are there beautiful moments along the way? Yes, of course! I will not deny God's amazing daily provision and His supernatural protection over us in many situations, and the joy I feel when I see these precious children's lives restored. I treasure these wonderful times. And my marriage to Jason is solid and we love and value each other deeply, each one helping the other to reach new potentials in our ministries and to obey the Lord's calling.

But when I go out, I go out in Jesus' name, knowing that my life is in His hands and no-one else's. Again, I don't say this for

---

18. Luke 9:23, NASB

my own glory. My life goal is only to be a willing vessel in the Lord's hands and to have Him receive me at the end with the words, "Well done, good and faithful servant."[19]

Now I don't know when the time of my departure will be, but I know our lives are fleeting on this earth and that Jesus can call me home at any time. So I'm going to keep doing what I know He wants me to do, till that day comes: make one more rescue.

Which is how I ended up back in Chiapas.

---

19. Matthew 25:21, NKJV

CHAPTER TWENTY-ONE

Chiapas: Light Into Darkness

But whoever has this world's goods, and sees his brother in need, and shuts up his heart from him, how does the love of God abide in him? - 1 John 3:17 (NKJV)

Compassion means going directly to those people and places where suffering is most acute and building a home there. - Henri Nouwen

IN MY YEARS serving the Lord through the Village Children's Home in Puebla, I thought I could say I'd seen and heard everything under the sun regarding the abuse and trafficking of children. But in early February 2022 I went through the most mind-boggling time of my entire life.

I received a phone call and then some forwarded texts from Maighel, a godson of mine who was in touch with people working with a ministry that helps persecuted Christians in Mexico. The messages came from the southern state of Chiapas, and they were terrifying. They spoke of homes being burned to the ground, kidnappings, rapes, beatings, shootings, murders, imprisonment on false charges, tortures, and so much more. Extreme church persecution. Erasing all traces of the deceased, as if they'd never existed. It was a Narco war - one in which evangelical Christians were the enemy for not conforming to the lifestyle of the local traditions or to the drug traffickers who were violently entering communities and taking over. And the police and the authorities? Nowhere to be seen.

"What do you think, Sister Nicole? Could you check it out?" Maighel asked me over the phone. (It may make you laugh - and it does me, too! - but this has happened often. Grown men, often authorities, call and ask me to scout things out because I have a lot of experience in this area. They say, "We don't know anyone else who has taken on the Narcos like you have, so we thought you might look into it for us.") It was hard to believe this was once again taking place in Mexico, but something inside me knew it was true. I decided I would, indeed, check it out.

Two days later, Jason, my attorney Gustavo, and I boarded a plane to Tuxtla Gutiérrez, Chiapas, just a few hours from the border of Guatemala. For Jason and me, it felt like coming full circle as we drove up the curved highway into San Cristóbal de las Casas, that incredibly colorful and multicultural city where we had been right before my car wreck back in 1993. It was where the Zapatistas had had their uprising and are still, to this day, solidly in charge of a number of nearby rural communities. In this case, the people we went to help spoke Tzotzil and Tseltal, indigenous languages from the mountainous highlands known as *Los Altos* that surrounded San Cristóbal.

We met with Noemi and Alex, who were trying to help the persecuted Christians. They explained to us the situation and became our friends. A little after that we met the son and daughter of a pastor who had been recently imprisoned. They confirmed it - the report I'd been given was all true. Before becoming a Christian, the pastor used to be involved in politics, but when he was saved he quit the life of empire-building and corruption that went with the politics. For a time, because of his prior influence and reputation, he was able to defend Christians from being falsely accused for crimes - a common occurrence in southern Mexico, as they are the least protected group of people. But then the tables turned: now he was imprisoned, also falsely accused of crimes he did not commit.

Over the next few days I heard and saw unimaginable things. I sat in a dark wooden shack with a hard dirt floor, listening to women and children tell me - in tears - graphic details that I simply could not fathom.

One of the Christian families had been fleeing their town, pursued by attackers who were hell-bent on running them down. The father, carrying his 4-year-old son in his arms, was caught and shot by the attackers, then hacked to death with machetes and burned, right in front of his son. The little boy, Charlie, managed to escape, and was found later by his distraught mother. Charlie was totally traumatized when I met him, unable to smile or respond to anyone.

The families who had fled the persecution had no beds, just boards and dirty blankets. There were 19 people crammed into two rooms in a tiny shack. Three small containers of food that were supposed to feed everyone.

I was taken to a women's prison not far from the city, a drab, concrete block building with white painted bars. In that place, justice could take years to be carried out. I wept as I listened to my Christian sisters' stories of being separated from their babies. They showed me the marks where bullets were still inside their bodies. They spoke of their anguish for their husbands, who they knew were being tortured and starved in a different prison hours away.

It was impossible for me to sit back and do nothing. I rallied supporters via social media in order to raise funds for our brothers and sisters. The very next day we bought them beds, blankets, food, and hygiene supplies. I quickly found two houses for rent: a five-bedroom house for the Christian refugees, and a smaller one that could be used as a base of operations for us. The refugee home quickly grew to accommodate 26 people: most were children who were currently motherless, and a couple of other adults.

I couldn't stay long. I returned to Puebla and then flew back and forth to Chiapas every other week, in order to buy food and supplies, establish some basic rules and norms for the house, and provide a full-time psychologist for the families and a teacher for the children.

During this time I met the regional director for the department for child and family welfare (DIF) in Chiapas, and discovered that some of the children and their cases had already been registered with them. The regional director and I were more than a little wary of each other. I'd heard fear-mongering stories about the DIF in Chiapas, that it was an unreliable institution riddled with corruption and evil people; meanwhile, the regional director had no idea who I was or what I was attempting to do with the families in San Cristóbal. She assumed and suspected the worst, her ideas fueled by rumors that I was a wealthy American who'd come to kidnap the children and sell them on the black market. We didn't hit it off so well at the beginning, to say the least.

Over the next few weeks we saw the situation with the persecuted Christians through to the point where another charity organization was able to take over and look after these families. We were ready to leave Chiapas and head back to Puebla for the last time. By this time we'd begun to establish better lines of communication with the DIF and come to have a much healthier mutual respect for each other's work.

And the DIF begged us not to leave.

The regional director began to share with me the types of cases they were confronted with daily. It broke my heart to hear them: cases of child sex trafficking, child pornography, rampant incest, abuse, abandonment, children who were victims of war, orphaned and alone.

There were other situations here that we didn't face so much in Puebla. Migrant children from Central America, escaping violence or looking for their parents who had traveled to the USA, would arrive in Chiapas with no identification and no protection, and would often be taken by evil people and forced into sexual exploitation. I learned that over 5,000 boys and girls are caught in a web of trafficking in the border zones of Chiapas and Guatemala.[24] Then I discovered that Chiapas is considered one of the worst places *in the world* in terms of child prostitution.[25]

"Señora Nicole, please stay," she implored me. "We have so many children who need a safe home to go to while their cases are being sorted out and justice is done. And there is nowhere for them to go. We have no more space at the State Home - and it's hours away from us. Please start a children's home here. We've seen your heart and we know you can help."

I wasn't sure what to do. I sought advice, and wrote to a missionary friend who'd lived and served in Chiapas for decades; he was one of those whom Freedom Ministries had been evacuating during the Zapatista uprising when I'd had my accident. I knew he could give me advice about coming down to this region of Mexico. He listened to what I told him and what I wanted to do. I was expecting him to be very encouraging, considering the need. His reply jolted me to the core.

"Nicole, the people down here have a whole different mindset. They're *nothing* like anyone else. They're ruthless and wicked, Nicole. I do not recommend you come down here. They will betray you and stab you in the back. The drug cartels can be brutal bastards. The indigenous people can be brutal, too. You don't want this to affect your other work. I suggest you pack your bags and go back to Puebla. I know there's a lot of suffering down here, but you have no idea what these people are like."

I realized this was another crossroads moment for me. Should I heed the advice of this brother, who had so many years of experience ministering in Chiapas and whom I respected? I could hear his heart and knew he didn't want me to get hurt, betrayed or killed by coming down here and exposing myself to the risks involved in rescuing children in such a dark place.

But by now, my own heart was invested in the needs I saw around me. I'd heard some of the stories that the DIF regional director had shared with me - and, as I write, they continue to happen. The migrant children are being taken and used for sex trafficking; many little girls and boys are being sexually abused by their own family members - fathers, brothers, grandfathers, uncles - and others are rented out daily to men by their own parents. A number of children are simply abandoned by their parents who are addicted to drugs or alcohol, or physically abused and tortured in ways we cannot comprehend. Children as little as 18 months and 2 years old. This is not just theory; it is happening right now.[26]

We'd go to restaurants to eat, and street children would come to my table and ask me for a *peso* (a Mexican coin). I would sit them next to me and order them a meal, while all the other diners would gasp. I'd ask them questions and listen to their stories as they quietly answered. Their parents had been killed or were "gone", so they lived with impoverished grandmothers who let them beg on the streets because they couldn't care for them, or with uncles who exploited them to work by day and raped them by night, or with other men and women who had taken them from their home towns and used them as they wished. Although these children hadn't eaten, they couldn't stay with me long. They were being watched by their traffickers.

I saw many children working in rough conditions - in the fields under the hot sun, walking the streets of San Cristóbal, cleaning windscreens at traffic lights - all of them with the same haunted look of children who wished they could eat, play, feel safe, and rest, but who could not do any of these things. They were hungry, tired, helpless and afraid.

Then there was the other side of the coin: the abusers. Once while walking on a narrow stone sidewalk in the center of San Cristóbal where the tourists hung out, I overheard two young men who were walking in front of me. As soon as I heard them talking, I knew they were American tourists. One was bragging to the other about the little indigenous teenage prostitute he'd had sex with the night before, and the things he did to her. The other agreed that this was a great place to do whatever you wanted with the native girls here - that he'd definitely be coming back next year. My whole body seethed as I heard their conversation. This was the underworld of Chiapas revealed to me - people from my own country coming to exploit young girls for their sick sexual pleasure and someone else's financial gain.

I realized that there was a battle raging in Chiapas for the children. The darkness was heavy and palpable - especially in some nearby towns in which veneration of saints and idolatry went hand in hand with animal sacrifice, machismo and extreme violence. You could feel the hostile atmosphere upon arrival; it was like a slap in the face as soon as you left your vehicle. The women did not smile. Most of the young teenage girls were carrying babies, wrapped up in their shawls on their backs.

I remembered the story of Queen Esther. Her words to Mordecai, before she went to meet with the King, turned over and over in my head: "*If I perish, I perish.*"[20] Was I prepared to die in order to rescue one more child? I knew I was.

So I did it. I started a new children's home in Chiapas. I'm so grateful to the Lord's Holy Spirit in confirming this new step, as well as my amazing family, our wonderful mission organization (since 2019 this has been Mountain Gateway, an awesome ministry with our tireless friends Britt and Audrey Hancock at the helm), extraordinarily generous donors, and newfound friends and helpers. I found people from nearby churches and even from other states who were willing to work as paid staff and volunteers, rented a large house in a quiet area of San Cristóbal, and on April 22, 2022 we inaugurated the Chiapas Children's Home (CCH). We were honored to have some very important state authorities present, and were welcomed beyond measure by them all.

The District Attorney made a short speech. "You are an answer to our prayers. We have nowhere to put the many children who have no safe place to live, and no-one to care for them. We are very grateful for your presence here in Chiapas."

A week later, Child Protection authorities began calling us daily, with new cases. And it's been non-stop ever since. Every single day.

People who cared for me said to me, "Nicole, this is not your battle."

I had to reply, "But it is, now. It is."

* * *

CCH has been going for about 2 years at the time of writing. With the amazing help of the DIF and state authorities, we've successfully rescued over 100 children from 8 different nations - Brazil, Haiti, Honduras, Nicaragua, El Salvador, Guatemala, Mexico, and - yes, even from the United States. Has it been easy

---

20. Esther 4:16, NASB

running a children's home in Chiapas while I live in Puebla and continue to take care of up to 60 rescued children at a time at VCH? It's been a MASSIVE challenge, much bigger than anything I could have imagined, with unexpected twists and turns.

There have been internal pressures. Especially at the beginning, a multicultural staff with their own ways of communicating (and more often, not communicating) caused tension. Rumors and gossip start up quickly if they are not checked. Finding the right people who are committed to serving the Lord and the children, while being willing to move and live in the southernmost state of Mexico, has not been easy. Gradually, though, we have built up a solid team of caring people who are working with each other's strengths and being Jesus' hands and feet to the hurting children who arrive.

There are also moments of great crisis among the children that reflect the trauma they arrive with and continue to process and heal from. Many of them arrive trembling and in tears, afraid of this new place, expecting to be treated badly, still carrying bruises and even stitches from the abusive environments they were pulled out of. If I can not be physically present in Chiapas when new children arrive, I always make a video call with them so as to help alleviate their fears, saying the same things to them as always: *You are loved. You are valued. You are safe. You will never be hurt here. We're your new family. Nothing that happened is your fault. You are not alone.*

There have been external pressures, too. One mother found the location of our rented home and turned up right outside the black metal doors, demanding her daughters back so she could prostitute them again to feed her own drug habit. Other parents try to slow down the justice system, putting in legal appeals that their children are "being mistreated" and forcing the district attorney and Human Rights representatives to visit the CCH week after week in order to prove that this is not the case.

Many times cases for justice drag on a lot longer than we would want them to, the children having to wait in tension and tears to find out what will happen to them and their aggressors.

And, horrifically, in some municipalities of Chiapas, the legal system allows both perpetrator and victim to be present in the courtroom at the same time, or for the child to listen to the voice and defense of the culprit - which is, as you can imagine, a massive trigger for all their traumas, fears and anxieties. It makes it that much harder for the children to recover emotionally.

The language barriers can also cause difficulties: Chiapas has 12 separate indigenous languages, and many of the children who arrive don't speak Spanish as their first language. We've cared for children of migrants from Central and South American countries who bring their own languages, cultures and personalities, on top of the severe trauma they've been through.

There is also the external tension of life in Chiapas. Even so many years after the Zapatista uprising, conflict and violence still exist in many regions. To make matters much worse, in the past few years two large drug cartels have entered and seized control of areas of Chiapas. "Self-defense groups" have set themselves up, supposedly to defend their towns, but who quickly turn against anyone who does not agree with all their violent actions - including Christians who do not wish to get involved with either group.

All of this causes us to be wary and careful as we travel to and fro. Christians are not seen as good people, like they are in many places around the world - they're seen as traitors. I've had to walk past a mob of angry young men shouting, "Here, the Narco traffickers are in charge! Away with the evangelical Christians! We're going to get rid of them all!"

Yes, Chiapas is definitely a different state, a sort of contemporary Wild West, a massive mix of people groups, social and economic situations, cultural norms and even religious beliefs that we find impossible to understand. And some of the stories that come out of this state make my blood boil.

* * *

KAREN

Little Karen, a quiet slip of a girl, lived in a nightmare world from the tender age of six. That was when her mother began to undress her so that her father could sexually abuse her in the "special room", in front of their altar built to worship *la Santa Muerte* (Holy Death).[27] In that evil place Karen was sadistically raped, over and over, for two years, in service to this demon.

At the age of eight, she was rushed to the hospital because her little body had begun to bleed profusely from the sexual abuse. On their way to the hospital, her father told her to lie to the doctors, to tell them that she was grabbed on her way to the store and raped by a stranger. Poor Karen passed out upon arrival, but regained consciousness while the doctor was attending to her.

Bravely, she told him the whole truth.

And, thankfully, justice was served. The court case lasted four years, but both her parents were sentenced to 70 years in prison. Karen was released from the state refuge she'd been living at for those four years - with nowhere to go. I was called and asked "if we could finish raising her". Of course, I said YES! Karen was brought to CCH where she could be safe, loved, and at peace.

* * *

BILLY

Billy was 12 but had the body of a six year old when we received him at CCH, trembling, thin and apprehensive. His life up to this point had been filled with terror and torture - the horrendous burn scars that covered his upper body and arms spoke volumes, scars he will live with forever - and indicative of the inner scars he carried from his abusive mother. Since his father disappeared, Billy had been banished to live with the farm animals, sleeping on the hard floor of the barn and receiving nothing but abuse from his mother and new stepfather.

There we found him, lying between two dirty thin blankets on the ground. Next to his "bed" were not toys and books, but buckets and pans, rakes and tools. He was forced to work daily, never going to school. Billy lived in one of those towns that had a reputation for violence and conflict. Yet it was finally the townspeople themselves that decided that Billy's abuse had to stop - and they made a collective plea for the authorities to step in and do something.

When we first met Billy, I noticed with shock that his file, held by the Child Protection authorities, was the size of an encyclopedia. I asked the legal representative how they could have so much information concerning Billy's case. Her reply shocked me even more: "We've known about Billy for 6 years now. But we couldn't remove him from his situation because we had no place to put him. There was no Mamá Nicole. Until now."

* * *

Stories like Karen's and Billy's seem implausible. We often think to ourselves, *This can't be true! How could anyone do such things to their own children? It's not humanly possible!* We are right to think this way. Our instinct is to reject such abuse and horrors as unnatural - and therefore, we think, impossible. Yes, it is unnatural; but it is not impossible. These are real cases, happening right now, and we *must* continue to rescue the children.

Even amidst the horrors we hear and the volatile situations that have become the norm in Chiapas, we have discovered an admirable quiet inner strength found in many adults and children in Chiapas - a steely force that helps them carry on and survive despite the most formidable obstacles of life. We see the perseverance of Christian brothers and sisters who face great opposition for deciding to follow Christ. Even when threatened with painful death and lifelong imprisonment (with torture), they do not deny His name. No, they are more than conquerors, seeking to bless and share God's word with those who oppose them. They look for ways to bring the light of Jesus to every child in the community.

When I reflect on all of this, I know God has not abandoned us. He does not change, and His heart continues to be with the children. I see His hand protecting us so many times, providing for the daily needs of the ever-growing numbers of children we take in, and guiding us in purchasing a block of land where we can build a home big enough for many children who can be rescued, restored and raised to know and love Him, their Heavenly Father.

CHAPTER TWENTY-TWO

Roots and Wings

But those who wait on the LORD Shall renew their strength; They shall mount up with wings like eagles, They shall run and not be weary, They shall walk and not faint. - Isaiah 40:31 (NKJV)

A wise woman once said to me that there are only two lasting bequests we can hope to give our children. One of these she said is roots, the other, wings. - Hodding Carter[28]

I DON'T KNOW who that wise woman was who said this to Hodding Carter; I wonder if it was his mom!

What does it mean to give our children roots and wings?

Roots are essential for a plant to grow and thrive, even in stormy weather. They hold the plant in place like an anchor. They protect plants from disease. And they allow the plant to grow by absorbing the air, water and nutrients from the soil and moving these up to the leaves which combine with sunlight.

A healthy family provides the strong roots that allow children to grow and thrive as well. A loving, safe environment, sufficient food, routine and discipline, and faith in our Creator

God and His Son Jesus Christ, allow children to withstand challenges and even crises throughout life.

This is what it means to give our children roots.

At first, a baby is totally dependent on its mother and father. Little by little, the older a child becomes, the more independence he/she can take on in life. At a certain age, the child is ready for school. Later comes sleepovers at the grandparents' home or at a friend's. They begin sports and cultural programs that allow them to discover their talents and hobbies.

And in later teenage years they begin to make bigger decisions on their own - what they want to study and be when they're older; how they can make a difference in the world; relationships, marriage, families of their own. As one of our rescued sons said to me years ago - "I was gonna be a gangster but now I am going to be a preacher!" Mistakes might be made, yes. But these are mitigated by resilience and determination to move forward.

This is what it means to give our children wings.

We don't force children to make those big life decisions when they are still infants. But neither must we suppress their instinct towards independence as they grow and mature. Each stage of life brings a new level of growth, and as parents or caregivers we need to encourage that growth - because this also brings hope. Hope that tomorrow will come, that I will be ready to face the new day, and that when the time comes I will be able to fly.

* * *

I look back at my own life, and see how in so many ways God was preparing me for the task set before me. He gave me a family who provided the roots that kept me strong and grounded throughout childhood and adolescence. They led me to do what Jesus spoke about in Matthew 25: feed the hungry, give water to the thirsty, take in the stranger, clothe the naked, and visit the sick and the imprisoned.

God gave me a husband who held fast to his promise "in sickness and in health", staying with me through that horrific wreck and the amnesia and recovery that followed. God guided Jason and me to the place where He would open my eyes to the need to rescue children from trafficking, giving me the opportunity to step out of my comfort zone and fly into a new world for which He had prepared me through all my life lessons.

Every child needs roots and wings. And every child who comes to the Village Children's Home, or the Chiapas Children's Home, needs them both as well. So many of them arrive with nothing but the clothes on their back and their physical and emotional traumas. Their brains have been wired through the period of their trauma to stay in survival mode: to do what they can just to stay alive, stay safe, and look after their younger siblings.

At the beginning they don't understand what a safe place is, or that now they'll have enough food to eat every day without having to go in search of it themselves or keep some of what they're given for tomorrow. Many don't have any frame of reference for love, or truth, or respect for others, because they were never given these things themselves.

And because they have no roots, neither are they looking forward to a future with hope. They are like the "bruised reed" that the prophet Isaiah spoke about.[21] Thank God - thank God for our Savior Jesus Christ, who does not break the bruised reed, nor snuff out the smoldering wick. He shows us what needs to be done to restore to these children what was lost.

It's because of the love of Jesus that we are here, rescuing one more, giving these beautiful children what they need in order for them to establish strong roots, grounded in His love, and

---

21. Isaiah 42:3

to stretch their wings at the right time and become all that they can be.

And this is what we do for them, as best we can, as long as they are with us, and for as long as God allows us to.

What Now?

He who testifies to these things says, "Surely I am coming quickly." Amen. Even so, come, Lord Jesus! - Revelation 22:20 (NKJV)

"You may choose to look the other way but you can never say again that you did not know." - William Wilberforce

WHAT IS GOD SAYING TO ME?

I'M SO HAPPY you've made it to the end of this book! It's not the end of my story - not until God calls me home. And you? What is your story? Take some time to reflect upon and pray about what you have read. What things have impacted you? What has God been speaking to you about? I encourage you to stop right now, write it down, and pray. Ask God to help you work through honestly what you might have to change in your own life - and for the strength to trust and obey Him fully. Write down your thoughts and what God is saying to you.

Since we began rescuing children and speaking out against

human trafficking, Tenango de las Flores - that town filled with darkness - has been transformed: policies have been put in place by authorities to make sure children are no longer trafficked there. And the state of Puebla is surging forward in producing laws that better protect children and adolescents, open the way to fostering and adoption, and deal justice to the sex offenders. Please know that it is God who gave me the strength and courage to move forward and do what He called me to do. And He will do the same for you! The world needs His people to be salt and light, to truly make a difference - will *you* do it?

If you have not already given your life to Jesus, I encourage you to do this. Come before God, believing in the death and resurrection of Jesus Christ to forgive your sins[29] and bring you to Him[30], while there is still time. Come to Him, willing to turn around and change those things in your life that don't please Him, and ask Him to transform you and make you a new person. You do not know how long you have on this earth; make your life right with God through Jesus before it is too late. As you've seen from my story, a relationship with God will not keep hardship and trauma from happening in your life; but He promises to be with you always, even to the very end of the age.[22]

* * *

I was once asked, "If God had shown you what would happen to you, would you still have said *yes*?" I paused just for a few moments, and then answered, "Yes, I would." The road might have been long and hard, but Jesus has proved He has been with me all the way. God is looking for people He can move through. He can do great things through you! All things are possible when you are yielded and submitted to God and committed to performing His will and purpose.

Ask God what He has planned for you. Whose lives is He

---

22. Matthew 28:20, NKJV

calling you to touch? Where is He calling you to go? What are the things He desires to do, in you and through you? Are you, like Esther, willing to obey and be used by Him? He has created you *for such a time as this*[23]. You are alive, this very day, because God has work for you to do. He has other people watching you, gaining courage as they observe you walk faithfully through your daily ups and downs, trials and tribulations, situations and circumstances.

I'D LIKE TO HELP. HOW CAN I DO THAT?

Please *pray* for me and my husband Jason - and for the ministries God has entrusted to us. We need people who will faithfully lift us up in prayer before the Lord. You see, I still have many challenges. As I mentioned in chapter 19, there are times when I am physically and mentally weak. There are constant threats from hitmen and pimps. There is a need for more caregivers for the children, people who love the Lord and have experience in helping children with trauma. And there are constant financial needs in order to give the children all that they lack: food, clothing, shoes, schooling, medical/dental care, counseling, and recreation. Please pray that God will continue to provide all that is needed for His children, according to all His riches in glory.

Please also prayerfully consider partnering with The Village Global by supporting us financially. Whether it be the children's homes, the rehab centers or the work ministering to the national churches, all our work is run purely on the support of others and their generous giving. It is quite possible that YOU may be the answer to your prayers for God's provision! Details on how to do this are below, through Mountain Gateway or The Village Global's website:

www.TheVillageGlobal.org

---

23. Esther 4:14

Many people have seen the 2023 movie *Sound of Freedom*, and wonder who is actually helping rescue children from traffickers and pedophiles. They have no idea where to even start looking, in order to support these efforts. You can also help us by reaching out to others through your social networks and churches, letting them know that there *are* people who are working hard to fulfill God's command to care for orphans and widows, and rescue those who are being taken away to death.[24] In this way, you give others the opportunity to partner in this work.

How can I protect those I love from trafficking?

It might be painful, but it's important to face up to the fact that human trafficking is real, and is affecting so many people's lives, including children and even infants. It might well be affecting people you know.

Sex trafficking in the age of the internet, especially after 2020, has increased dramatically. Online social interactions - whether it be through social media or online video games - easily entice vulnerable teenagers into unsafe relationships with strangers. Please educate yourself and your family so you can become aware and protect your loved ones from dangers and temptation.

If you have children, there are things you can do to keep them safe: stay in constant communication with them; monitor and establish limits for which online sites they visit and the social networks they use; know who is connecting with them; set rules for messaging, emailing, gaming, and using the webcam.[31] Help them become aware of the risks involved - and let them know they can always talk to you about anything strange.

Whether you do or don't have children, think about how you can help other children in your own area who may be at

---

24. Isaiah 1:17, Proverbs 11:14

risk of violence, abuse or trafficking. When you go out, become more aware of your surroundings. Who are your neighbors? What is happening at the local stores - are there children who are unattended? Have you seen children alone at traffic lights or on the streets? Look around you, and listen. If you see anything that does not look right, report it to 911 or Child Protection authorities - it may save that child's life.

We need to break the chain of child sex trafficking from both ends: we must stop those who kidnap/entice children, exploit them in work or prostitution or cause them physical harm; but we also need to stop ourselves and prevent our loved ones from being enticed into wrong relationships, or becoming trapped in purchasing and consuming pornography, which enslaves and degrades, continuing the cycle of child sex trafficking. This topic deserves an entire book in itself. But we *must* become a part of the solution, and not turn a blind eye to the problem.

* * *

A final word: if you have been a victim of sexual abuse, or are dealing with thoughts about suicide, please talk to someone. Get counseling. If you feel you have no-one who will listen to you, I will listen and connect you with people who can help. Please write to me at: nfitz321@yahoo.com

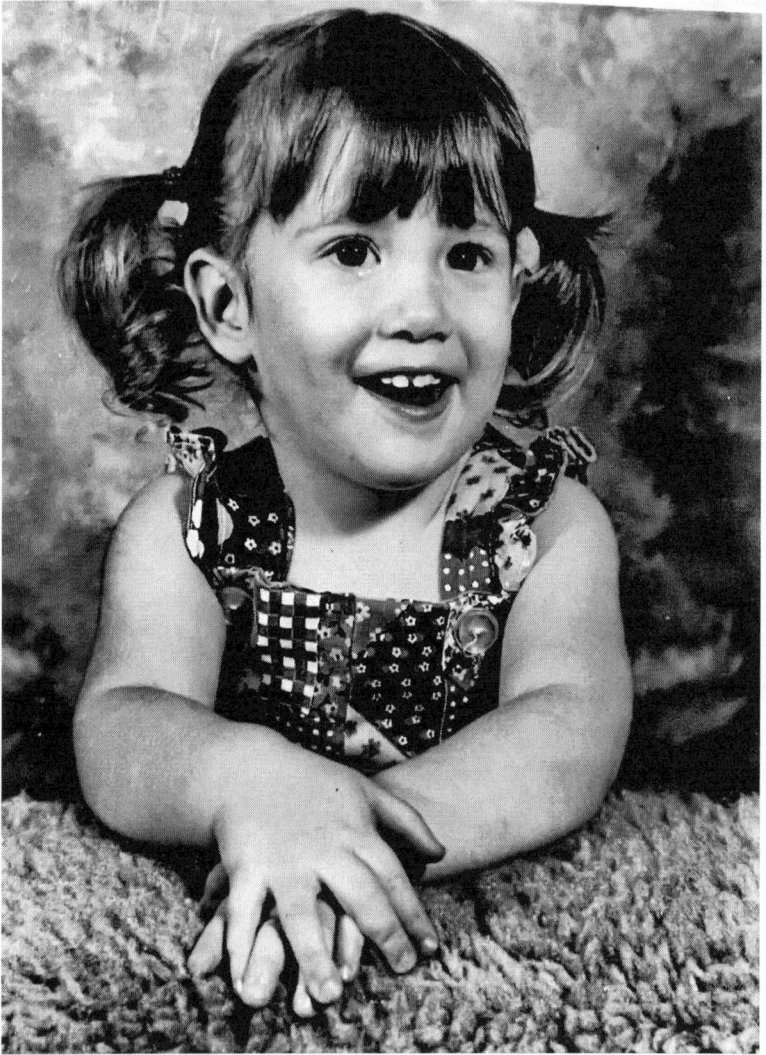

Nicole always hated taking pictures as a child ...
so chewing gum was her remedy

*Nicole and Jason's wedding meal next to their spiritual father,
David Hogan, Dec 1992*

Mason family portrait just days before the wreck, Dec 1993

The 1992 Dodge Cummins Diesel, totalled Dec 1993

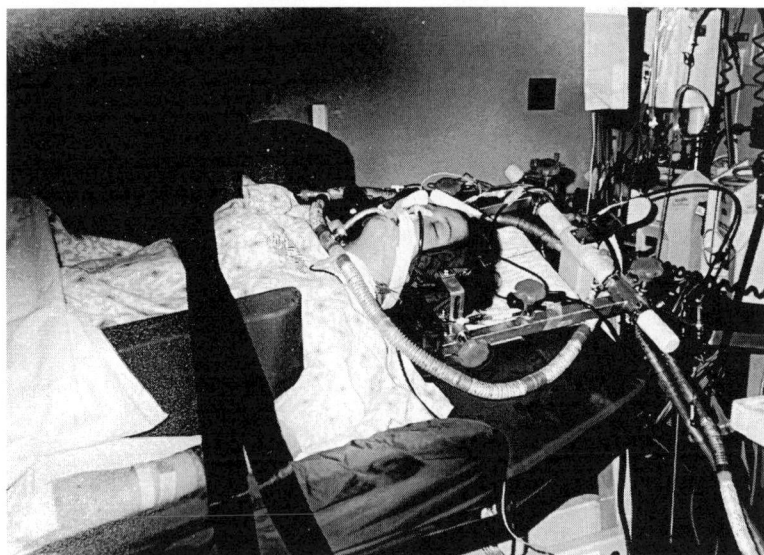

Nicole in ICU weeks after the accident, Jan 1994

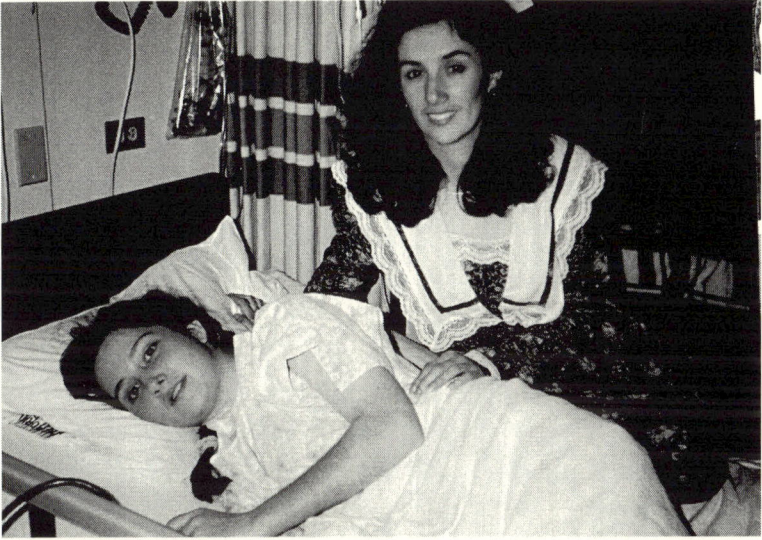

Nicole with her Mom once she was moved to her own room, late Feb 1994

Family picture, 1997: Nicole, Jason, Sed

Early years, driving through the mountains to take the Gospel to the indigenous tribes

Jason and Sed with the church planted in Pocantla, Hidalgo state

The Fitzpatrick home was always packed with house church members on Wednesday market days

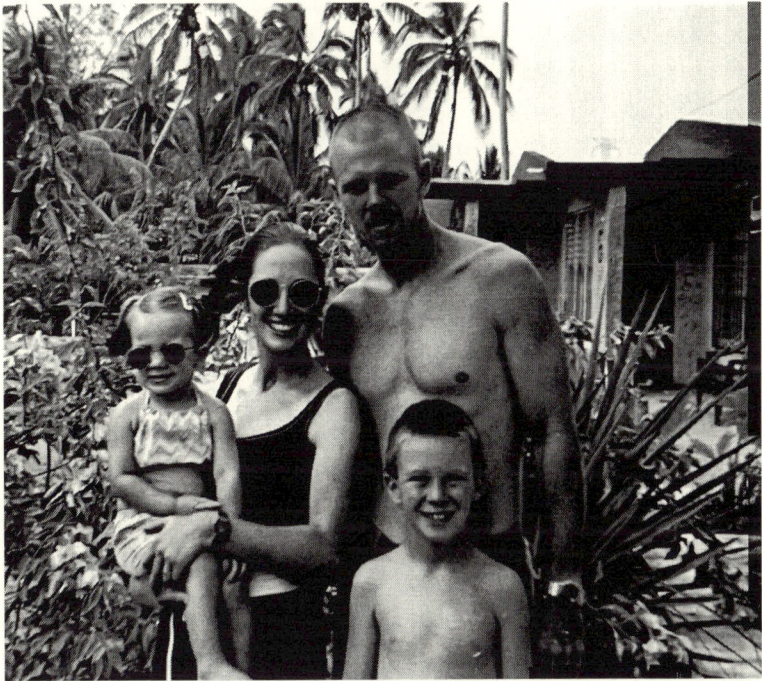

Enjoying time together as a family before the transition to Tenango de las Flores, May 2003

One of many thousands of converts Jason has baptized

Jasmine (front), always present and wanting to help, with some of Nicole's first rescues

A few of the hundreds of princesses the Fitzpatricks have been privileged to rescue and raise at VCH

A trip to the beach where the children go through the process of forgiveness and healing

Often there are tears when the rescued children are celebrated for the very first time

Loving on a few of the CCH boys

Each child is precious, loved and safe

Fitzpatrick family picture, Mar 2024

NICOLE FITZPATRICK was born in Baton Rouge, Louisiana. She is the child of missionary parents who served in Guatemala, Mexico, and Peru. Nicole married Jason in 1992. She fell in love with her husband twice: once before they got married, the second time a year later, when Nicole was in a shocking wreck and sustained multiple head and organ injuries. Suffering from amnesia when she awoke from her coma, she couldn't remember Jason, or anyone from her family. Jason went to work to win her heart a second time ... and succeeded.

Nicole and Jason have served together as missionaries in Mexico since 1992, sharing the gospel and planting churches in the rural mountains covering over 10 states in south-central Mexico. As she ministered to women and children, Nicole obeyed the call to rescue children from human trafficking. Since 2004, Nicole has rescued more than 2,000 children. She continues to live and work in Mexico with the support of her son and daughter and the protection of her Rhodesian Ridgebacks.

For more information, visit:
www.TheVillageGlobal.org

Or write to:
info@mountaingateway.org

ENDNOTES

1. About Compassion International | Discover Our Mission. www.compassion.com/about/about-us.htm.
2. Freedom Ministries | Jesus Is King. freedom-ministries.us.
3. "Editorial De El Despertador Mexicano." Enlace Zapatista, 16 Sept. 2020, enlacezapatista.ezln.org.mx/1993/12/31/editorial-de-el-despertador-mexicano. Article in Spanish.
4. HaloFlight. "About | HaloFlight." HaloFlight | Nonprofit Air Ambulance Service of South Texas, 23 May 2023, haloflight.org/explore/about.
5. "United States of Mexico" is Mexico's official name. Constitución Política de los Estados Unidos Mexicanos [México], 5 Febrero 1917, available at: <https://www.diputados.gob.mx/LeyesBiblio/pdf/CPEUM.pdf> (Document in Spanish)
6. DIF = Desarrollo Integral de la Familia, or Comprehensive Family Development. Sistema Nacional DIF | Gobierno | gob.mx. www.gob.mx/difnacional/que-hacemos. Article in Spanish.
7. "General 5 — SAFE (Survivors Against Familial Exploitation)." SAFE (Survivors Against Familial Exploitation), www.safe4us.org/statistics.
8. "Definition of Human Trafficking." Merriam-Webster Dictionary, 9 Oct. 2023, www.merriam-webster.com/dictionary/human%20trafficking.
9. General Law on the Rights of Girls, Boys and Adolescents, Article IV: Right to Live in a Family. From https://www.cndh.org.mx/ni%C3%B1as-ni%C3%B1os/derechos-humanos-de-ninas-y-ninos (version in English available)
10. "What Is Birth Registration and Why Does It Matter?" UNICEF, www.unicef.org/stories/what-birth-registration-and-why-does-it-matter.
11. "Global Report on Trafficking in Persons 2022" United Nations Office on Drugs and Crime. https://www.unodc.org/documents/data-and-analysis/glotip/2022/GLOTiP_2022_web.pdf.

12. Universàl, Redacción El. 60% of World Child Pornography Produced in Mexico. El Universal, 20 Nov. 2016, www.eluniversal.com.mx/articulo/english/2016/11/19/60-world-child-pornography-produced-mexico-0.

13. Morales, Ana Paula. "Catholic Prevention Organization: Mexico Ranks First in Human Trafficking and Child Abuse." Catholic News Agency, 15 Oct. 2023, www.catholicnewsagency.com/news/254000/catholic-prevention-organization-mexico-ranks-first-in-human-trafficking-and-child-abuse.
México, Primer Lugar De La OCDE En Maltrato Infantil: Senador Martínez Martínez. comunicacion.senado.gob.mx/index.php/periodo-ordinario/boletines/15298-mexico-primer-lugar-de-la-ocde-en-maltrato-infantil-senador-martinez-martinez.HTML. Article in Spanish.
Both these articles state that "The Organization for Economic Cooperation and Development (OECD) stated in a January report that 'Mexico ranks first in child sexual abuse; first in exploitation, homicides, and trafficking of minors; and first in creation and distribution of child pornography.'"

14. Thorn. "Child Pornography and Sexual Abuse Statistics | Thorn." Thorn, 30 Aug. 2022, www.thorn.org/child-pornography-and-abuse-statistics.

15. Barrios, Carolina, et al. "How Human Trafficking Worsened in Mexico During COVID-19." InSight Crime, Oct. 2023, insightcrime.org/news/human-trafficking-worsened-mexico-covid.

16. "Online Grooming at 'Unprecedented Levels.'" Jersey Evening Post, 6 Aug. 2023, jerseyeveningpost.com/news/2023/08/06/online-grooming-at-unprecedented-levels.

17. See, for example, Deuteronomy 10:18; Deuteronomy 27:19; Psalm 10:14; Psalm 82:3; Matthew 25:35.

18. Wikipedia contributors. "Hurricane Earl (2016)." Wikipedia, July 2023, en.wikipedia.org/wiki/Hurricane_Earl_(2016).

19. "Crystal Methamphetamine: Fast Facts" National Drug Intelligence Center, USDOJ. https://www.justice.gov/archive/ndic/pubs5/5049/5049p.pdf

20. "What Is Vicarious Trauma? | the Vicarious Trauma Toolkit | OVC." Office for Victims of Crime, ovc.ojp.gov/program/vtt/what-is-vicarious-trauma.

21. Thomson Reuters Foundation. "Number of Women Human Traffickers 'Exceptionally High' -UN." news.trust.org, news.trust.org/item/20141124163933-6vy1j.

22. Elizabeth L. Jeglic PhD. "Understanding the Role of Women in Sex Trafficking" Psychology Today, https://www.psychologytoday.com/us/blog/protecting-children-sexual-abuse/202112/understanding-the-role-women-in-sex-trafficking

23. Bonhoeffer, Dietrich (2015). "The Cost of Discipleship", p.44, SCM Press

24. Niñez Migrante, Trat y Explotación Infantil en México. Temas Emergentes en la Agenda Nacional At https://appweb.cndh.org.mx/biblioteca/archivos/pdfs/Var_14.pdf Article in Spanish.

25. RIGHTS-MEXICO: 16,000 Victims of Child Sexual Exploitation. web.archive.org/web/20070814185049/http://www.ipsnews.net/news.asp?idnews=38872.

26. Del Sur, Marvin Bautista |. Diario. "La Pederastia Aumenta De Manera Considerable En Chiapas." Diario Del Sur | Noticias Locales, Policiacas, Sobre México, Chiapas Y El Mundo, www.diariodelsur.com.mx/local/la-pederastia-aumenta-de-manera-considerable-en-chiapas-9716404.html. (Article in Spanish)

27. This is a supposed "saint", although the Satanic connections are clear. See, for example:
Tucker, Duncan. "Santa Muerte: The Rise of Mexico's Death 'saint.'" BBC News, 1 Nov. 2017, www.bbc.com/news/world-latin-america-41804243.

28. Hodding Carter (1953). Where Main Street Meets the River. Page 337. Rinehart & Company, New York.

29. "... that if you confess with your mouth Jesus as Lord, and believe in your heart that God raised Him from the dead, you will be saved; for with the heart a person believes, resulting in righteousness, and with the mouth he confesses, resulting in salvation." Romans 10:9-10, NASB

30. "For Christ also suffered for sins once for all time, the just for the unjust, so that He might bring us to God …" 1 Peter 3:18, NASB

31. Task Force, Trafficking in America. "Online Exploitation of Children and Grooming - Trafficking in America Task Force." Trafficking in America Task Force, Aug. 2020, traffickinginamericataskforce.org/online-exploitation.

Read about: Gladys Aylward
William Wilberforce
"You may choose to look the other way, but you can never say again that you did not know."